Letterheads
&
Business
Cards

Editor
Chris Foges

Letterheads
&
Business
Cards

A RotoVision Book
Published and Distributed
by RotoVision SA
Rue Du Bugnon 7
CH-1299 Crans-Près-Céligny
Switzerland

RotoVision SA
Sales and Production Office
Sheridan House
112–116a Western Road
Hove. BN3 1DD UK

Tel: +44 (0)1273 72 72 68
Fax: +44 (0)1273 72 72 69
E-Mail: Sales@RotoVision.com

Distributed to the trade in the
United States by:
Watson-Guptill Publications
1515 Broadway
New York. NY 10036
USA

10 9 8 7 6 5 4 3 2 1

ISBN 2-88946-390-4

Book designed by Struktur Design

Production and separations
in Singapore by
ProVision Pte. Limited

Tel: +65 334 7720
Fax: +65 334 7721

Contents

Introduction

Johannes Baptiste de Taxis was looking for a way to make some money, and hit upon the idea of unifying Europe's postal routes and running them as a commercial operation. In 1519, Holy Roman Emperor Maximillian 1 made him Postmaster General, and a new communication age was born. The date doesn't mark the birth of letter writing, or for that matter letterheads, however. Letter writing dates from pre-history, and the use of unique piece of design on which to write them is not much younger: even trade cards – a fore-runner of the business card – pre-date the Postmaster General; one of the earliest known examples is for a hatter in Paris and dates from around 1470.

Before Maximillian's creation of a unified postal system, written correspondence in Europe was mainly between kings, diplomats and the like, and confined to national or international politics, although by the 15th century the growth of trade between commercial towns had led to an increase in written communications on what might loosely be described as prototype letterheads. By the 17th and 18th centuries, however, merchants, trades guilds and the like had their own letterheads, similar to those of today in many respects, and notable principally for their ornate decorative splendour.

It was not for another hundred years, though, that the post, and with it the letterhead, became central to business as well as personal communications. In 1840, Sir Rowland Hill introduced a flat charge of one penny for any letter, sent anywhere within Britain. The new postal charges were immediately taken advantage of by groups such as the Anti Corn Law League, who recognised a new and effective way to disseminate propaganda. Today, a wide variety of organisations including big corporations, small businesses and private individuals still use the letter as one of their most effective and direct forms of communication.

Even in the age of the fax and e-mail, the UK's Royal Mail still deals with nearly forty million business letters a day, while the US Postal Service has grown significantly since Benjamin Franklin was made its first Postmaster General in 1775: it now delivers hundreds of millions of items every day to eight million businesses and 250 million Americans. The letter has some particular and distinctive design qualities that give it an edge over other forms of communication: receiving a letter is a visual treat with colour, images and typography working harmoniously. It is a sensuous experience – most letters are printed on high-quality stocks; they are folded and inserted in envelopes giving the impression of substance and three-dimensionality. Put together in stages, signed and sent, the letter gives it a feeling of permanence and credibility that other forms of communication do not have. As a punning advertising slogan for the UK's Royal Mail has it, 'People respond to a letter'.

08 09

The designer's role
The graphic designer, as we understand the term today, only became involved with letterhead design in the 1920s. Printed letterheads engraved with a seal or symbol became common by the 18th century, and by the 19th century business stationery had developed significantly, although its design was still in the hands of printers, who would customise designs for clients from a range of ready-made alphabets and images from catalogues. Many carried an illustration of the firm's physical assets – its factory or offices – as a graphic boast. These letterheads, while attractive and functional, were essentially formulaic, and thus a different proposition from that offered by independent design consultants throughout the 20th century. That notwithstanding, many printers continue to offer the service of letterhead design – several hundred even offer a complete service through the Internet, where the relevant information is taken on-line and formatted electronically into pre-existing templates.

But at the turn of the century, the growth in advertising and packaging brought with it a recognition that all of the visual communications material issued by a company were representative of it, and each should be considered on its own merits. This catalysed a change in the approach to letterhead design, and we begin to see the basics of branding, or what is now referred to as corporate identity, on printed stationery: that is to say, the use of a group of typefaces, a selection of colours and images, and a logo. By the 1920s, freelance design consultants were regularly designing letterheads and business cards for clients, and the design of stationery, often as part of a larger corporate identity programme, had become economically important to the design industry.

Also active in the 1920s was Jan Tschichold, a young German designer who was influenced by the teachings of Walter Gropius and the Bauhaus school, and showed how the ideas put forward there could work in the area of communications, rather than architecture and furniture design.

The graphic design work being done by members of the European Avant Garde in art such as El Lissitzky, Herbert Bayer and Kurt Schwitters was 'formalised' in Tschichold's 1928 book, 'Die Neue Typographie' ('The New Typography'), in which he laid out the modernist rationale for design. In a chapter devoted to business forms, Tschichold presented the letterhead as a working piece of information design, in which its various components played an active role in synchrony with the contents of the letter itself, as opposed to performing a largely decorative role. Tschichold's theorising on letterheads was set in the context of an increasingly industrialised, business-led society. Modernist designers debated the role and function of design in the context of industry, and rejected the old 'artistic' designs as being out of step with the character of the world they were working in. While some of his orthodoxies regarding absolutes and standards were later challenged, Tschichold's basic assertion that the role of the designer in design for business was the clear and effective communication of information holds true today.

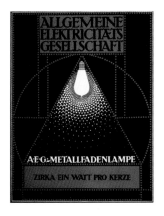

Corporate identity
This emphasis on standards and uniformity also fed into
the concurrently growing practice of corporate identity
making – the idea that a company or organisation must
have a strong and coherent visual identity to act as an
expression of its 'personality'. This had been on
companies' – and designers' – agendas since the turn
of the century. In 1907, the architect Peter Behrens was
commissioned to overhaul the visual identity,
communications and even buildings of the German
electrical firm AEG, in what is widely reckoned to be the
first major corporate identity job.

At its most basic, a corporate identity is achieved through
the design of a mark or logo, by which the company and
its products might be recognised. This mark can then be
applied, in a controlled way, to all of the company's
communications – its brochures, its advertising, its
packaging and, of course, its stationery.

Some of the more unusual
components of the modern
stationery system. Design
by The Attik

Letterhead and identity manual for
the Royal College of Art, London,
designed by Alan Kitching at the
Typography Workshop

A company has a variety of audiences, and it also has a variety of things it wants to tell them – sometimes individually, sometimes collectively. For collective communication, a company might advertise or create a brochure. For individual communications on a wide variety of topics, however, the basic 'big three' of stationery systems – the letterhead, business card and compliments slip are suitable for most purposes. The company will probably also have at its disposal other branded communication tools, designed in synchrony with the letterhead: the envelope or gummed envelope label, the fax header, the invoice, the credit note, the order confirmation, sticky labels for floppy disks, CD-ROMs, video cassettes – the family of letterhead relations continues to grow. (Meanwhile, other items of stationery decline in importance: as more records are kept on computer, fewer rolodex-compatible business cards are required, for example. Similarly, visiting cards, as distinct from business cards, have largely disappeared in the last fifty years.)

The ways in which the items in a company's 'communications tool kit' are used are dictated by an identity manual produced by the designer – a set of guidelines which ensure that each item works in the way that it was intended. The letterhead section of an identity manual, for example, should tell the user where on the sheet to put the recipient's address, how far down the sheet to start typing, how far in from the left-hand side, and where to stop on the right. In some cases it might contain stylistic recommendations such as whether to use numerals or words for numbers, how to write dates and percentages, or even how to sign a letter. The following extract from an identity manual produced in the 1960s for British Rail by Design Research Unit shows the level of detail included in some manuals. 'Where there is room, leave six spaces for the written signature and then type the name of the sender with his or her designation on the line below. The designation is not necessary where it is printed at the head of the paper. Name and designation may be omitted where the letter is informal.'

Selection of business cards
designed by the Japanese design
consultancy Azone & Associates

12 13

Form and function
As a communications tool for a company or individual,
the letterhead has three basic functions: primarily, of
course, it is a means to convey a message. Secondarily,
it clearly presents a small amount of useful information
concerning that company, and the information contained
within the letter: who it came from, where it came from,
how it relates to other correspondence and so on. The
Japanese designer Takenobu Igarashi has suggested
that the clear presentation of such information may
explain why the Japanese attach great importance to the
exchange of business cards at the start of a meeting:
the Japanese language uses over 7,000 symbols, the
most common being Kanji, which can be hard to
differentiate as many words with identical pronunciations
may have very different meanings, so that one can only
be sure of understanding something correctly when it is
seen written down.

大
塚
孝
博

t

BIN ŌFUSA

大
房

敏

Takahiro Otsuka │ 03 5467 4710 │ Fax. 03 5467 4712

Interior Architecture

Telephone
(03)37.97.67.90

Facsimile
(03)37.97.64.05

Akimi Okazaki

Soichi Mizutani Design Office Co.,Ltd.
3FC BOX-8, 4-24-10
Minami Aoyama, Minato-ku
Tokyo 107 Japan

Letterhead with information relating to ownership, location and status. Design by Alan Dye and Associates

Letterhead detail: information relating to the profession of the sender. Design by Thomas Manss and Company

The letterhead or business card may well also give some form of professional provenance: it is common for those with professional qualifications to include them on letterheads and business cards. Furthermore, in the UK for example, it is a legal requirement that the letterhead carry a certain amount of information relating to the ownership, location and status of the company: the registered office of any limited company must be shown, as must the directors of any company registered under the 1916 Companies Act.

More rules exist for sole traders working under their own names, more for those working under other names, and yet more still for invoices or credit slips.

In addition a company might want to describe its business – even if it is just to say 'architect' or 'accountant'. A subtler, less literal description of the business is often achieved through the use of illustration – from the company's own mark to a specially created design that tells the reader something more about the 'personality' of the company – perhaps that it is fun to work with; that it is successful; that it is forward looking. In this respect, it is only in degrees of sophistication that letterheads have changed at all since the status symbols of the last century.

Instruction sheet from
Jan Tschichold's Typografische
Entwurfstechnik (1932). The folded
transparent vellum sheet shows
a practical example overlaid with
DIN guidelines

The rules of letterhead design
As has been described, there are certain elements which
all letterheads share, and others that are unique to each
company or individual. The designer's job is to combine
them in a way that is of greatest benefit to their client. A
conflict does exist between the standard and the
unique. The market, and human nature, value the
unique and bespoke: they attract attention and give
pleasure to the mind and the eye. Yet, on the other
hand, design thinkers from Eric Gill to the Bauhaus
school have argued that where the designer is working
for industry, he should adopt its qualities of precision,
utility and rationality, and work to a set of standards
recognised and accepted by all.

While there are no rules apart from those enshrined in
law, as described earlier, there are standards and
precedents. No law says that a letterhead must be a
particular size or shape, but a set of precedents and
nationally recognised standards means that most are.
The Japanese letterhead usually measures twenty-one
by twenty-six centimetres; the American is eight and a
half by eleven inches. The Europeans use the Deutsche
Industrie Normen (or DIN) system, devised in Germany
the early 1920s. The European letterhead size A4 – which
at 297 x 210 millimetres is the 476 Standard – refers to
this system, which was later adopted by the International
Standards Organisation in Switzerland. Business cards
are A7 in the DIN system, or 105 x 74 millimetres, while
envelope sizes are covered by the C series.

The designers of the DIN system are often referred to as architects, perhaps out of respect for the mathematical simplicity, yet bold brilliance of their creation.

The ratio of the lengths of the size of any DIN paper size is one : the square root of two, meaning that however many times the paper is folded, the ratio remains the same. In his translation of Jan Tschichold's 'The New Typography', the design writer Ruari McLean makes the point that DIN's roots as a system for architects and engineers was a great part of its appeal for modernist designers such as Tschichold: it puts the less technical, more arbitrary practice of graphic design on the same formal footing as three-dimensional, engineering-based design.

While designers are free to disregard national standards, they should only do so after some thought: paper is now produced in standard sizes, and deviating from that may create the need for a bespoke sheet. Similarly, most of today's companies use software and hardware set up by the manufacturer to anticipate standards, from the word processing package to the desktop printer. Again, deviation from the norm can result in expense and time wasting.

Various influential designers and movements have argued about what belongs on the face of a letterhead, in what form, and in what place. Designers associated with the Bauhaus rejected all illustration except for simple geometrical shapes in primary colours. In 'The New Typography', Jan Tschichold proposed such standards as the use of asymmetric layouts, sans serif type and a wide left-hand margin. The British designer Herbert Spencer, in his book 'Design for Business Printing' (1952), argued that there were two sorts of printing – utility and promotional. As conveyors of information rather than advertisements, letterheads fall into the former category and should therefore be designed with clarity in mind. Furthermore, Spencer observed that letterheads should be easy to file and retrieve, recommending that information which would help these processes be placed on the right-hand side of the sheet. It is up to the individual designer, in the knowledge of the requirements of their client and the circumstances of their time, whether they pay any heed to these suggestions, but precedent is a powerful force and in most letterheads produced today, the influence of history is clear.

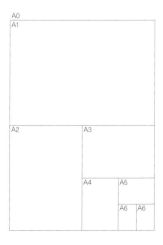

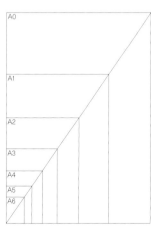

CJS Plants business card,
illustration printed on both front
and reverse faces, designed by
The Partners

The challenge of the new
Letterhead design used to fall into the category of what
was known as 'jobbing printing'. The name says about
it what many people still believe: that in design terms
letterheads are by definition formulaic and dull. On the
first point, as FHK Henrion wrote in 1967, "the visual
coordination of stationery is easy to begin, and very
hard to finish". To which one might reply with a quote
from another design great, Java pioneer Ed Frank:
"I think there are two types of people in this world –
people who can start things and people who can finish
things. And while I place great value on the finishers,
it's the starters who are rare because they can envision
what isn't there."

Charles Short

CJS Plants
Avery Hill Nursery
Avery Hill Park
Bexley Road
London SE9 2PG
Tel 081-850 1110
Fax 081-850 2110
Mobile Phone
0860 335417

De Stijl NB. Letterhead designed
by Theo Van Doesburg in 1920,
printed letterpress

The European designers of the avant garde, present at the birth of graphic and typographic design as a discipline in its own right, certainly envisioned what wasn't there and shaped the way we think about design and its function even today. And they used the humble letterhead to communicate new and revolutionary ideas about design, proving that far from being formulaic, the letterhead is an ideal breeding ground for innovation and experiment. Letters sent between the leading practitioners in Poland, France, Germany, Holland and the US carried on their faces the living evidence of a shift in design thinking. The flow of letters not only spread the influence of these schools of thought, but helped define their development.

Letterheads for the various movements of the time such as the Bauhaus school, and others which were not even physical entities such as Futurism, Constructivism and Dada, were the primary means of communicating and recording the significant changes taking place in the ways that designers were approaching visual communication. What those designers showed was that as well as being a test of skill, letterhead design can also be bold, beautiful and significant. It is up to the designer today, with the tools at his disposal – the choice of materials, form, printing and surface effects, illustration and typography – to carry on that tradition of graphic innovation.

A bespoke watermark in a letterhead sheet, created by Arjo Wiggins Fine Papers

Plastic business card for and by multimedia design studio AMX

Plastic business card in the style of a credit card, for use at a John Galliano fashion show. Design by Area

Metal business card designed and produced by the Graphic Metal Company

Business card designed by and for Sagmeister Inc. The letter 'S' is revealed when the card sits fully inside its transparent sheath

Materials

As Ernst Lehner noted in his book 'The History of the Letterhead', paper is a relative newcomer to the game of letter writing. Although the first sheet was made in China in about 200 BC, there was a time when it was not viable to send letters on paper, and communications were sent on Sumerian bricks, Assyrian and Babylonian clay tablets, Egyptian papyrus, Greek sheepskin, Roman wax tablets and a myriad of other devices. It goes without saying, of course, that today's letterheads and business cards will almost invariably be printed on paper of one sort or another. But even within paper, there is an almost infinite variety available to the designer: uncoated papers, coated papers, translucent papers, coloured stocks, hand-made papers and a host of others offer an enormous variety of choice, the making of which is a fundamental part of the design process. Some materials lend themselves better than others to certain printing processes or special effects, but for letterheads the designer is by no means restricted to what are known as office papers.

There are also positive client benefits to be had from the right choice of stock, beyond an impressive look and feel to the letterhead: for an order of a few thousand sheets and upwards, a bespoke stock is a very real option, economically. A sheet containing a bespoke watermark, or other features such as microfibres embedded in the paper, can provide the client with with a degree of security.

Business card for the book
publisher Faber & Faber. Design
by Frost Design

Business card designed by and
for the Conran Design Group. The
card comes inside a metal folder
which also carries a mini-portfolio
of the company's work

Form

Graphic design is often wrongly thought of as two-dimensional design: on closer inspection, however, it is obvious that books, magazines, brochures and indeed letterheads operate in three dimensions – even the most basic letterhead is designed to be folded. Although, typically, a letter is in the DIN A4 size (in the UK and Europe) or US Letter size in the US, is read portrait and is one unbroken sheet of paper with squared-off corners and neat cuts at the sides, the designer is able to change the format of the letter in a number of ways: through cutting, folding and changing the shape and size of the sheet.

This might be done to accommodate a particular type of information, or to allow the card/letterhead to be used for a dual purpose – or merely to make it more memorable, or to raise a smile from the reader.

While the standard fold into thirds allows the designer to feel sure that the address will end up in the right place for use with window envelopes, for example, using an alternative folding pattern can add life and a sense of functionality to a letterhead. It can act as a visual descriptor of the company's business, as in HGV's letterhead for Sutherland Building Services (pages 34-35), or be witty and amusing, as in The Partners' visually punning letterhead for Silk Purse (pages 42-43).

National standards notwithstanding, designers are also free to experiment with paper shape. As the pioneering Japanese designer Shigeo Fukada wrote in 'Letterheads of the World' (1977), 'letterhead paper shape should not have to be square to perform its function. It is not necessary to think about extreme cases like roundness or triangles, but I wish, by all means to use letter paper of parallelogram or rhomboid [shape].'

Business card for Pascal Wüest, a photographer. The address is applied with a rubber stamp. Design by Wild & Frey

Letterhead for Richard Foster. The company name is embossed down the side of the sheet. Design by Lippa Pearce

Letterhead and business card for Random Bus. The company's name is reflected in illustrations across the stationery system which show a 'random' selection of views of a bus. Design by Sagmeister Inc.

Surface effects

From the days of engraved trade cards, stationery designers have added character and a feeling of quality to the letterhead or business card with surface effects through printing techniques and treatments such as embossing, debossing, foils, varnishes and laminations.

Most letterheads are now litho printed but techniques such as letterpress, which was invented in the 1400s and was still the most prevalent in the 1920s and '30s, can create stunning effects. It is a distinctly 'low tech' approach but, like the rubber-stamped letterhead produced by Wild & Frey (below left), it has a certain charm and, in many instances, budgetary advantages. Some printers, such as Artomatic, whose own stationery system is featured later in this book, specialise in unusual print techniques or in printing on unusual materials. Even run-of-the-mill printers, however, should be able to cope with techniques such as embossing or foil blocking, which lend a sense of quality and distinction to a business card or letterhead.

Illustration

Since the earliest recorded examples in the fifteenth
century, letterheads have carried illustrations of one sort
or another. And while the type of illustration is dictated
by contemporary fashions and the limitations of printing
processes, generally speaking they are an integral
feature of the letterhead.

Here again, the options open to the designer are
numerous: at its most basic, the letterhead will probably
carry a company logo, but after that, the designer may
use hand-rendered illustration, photography, typographic
illustration or ideograms containing pertinent slogans
or messages.

Even in instances where it is desirable to leave as much
white space as possible on the face of the letterhead,
as current design aesthetics suggest in cases where
formality is a consideration, there is still an equal
amount of space on the reverse face which can be used
to carry further 'information' about the company in the
shape of illustration.

Letterhead for Celcius Films
with the address printed on the
reverse of the sheet. Design by
Carlos Segura of Segura Inc.

Letterhead for Martin Bax, the
editor of a poetry journal. Designed
by Alan Kitching of the Typography
Workshop and printed letterpress

Compliments slip for Planit
Events, an event planning
organisation. The date on which
the letter was sent is shown by
pushing out one of the scored
circles at the top of the sheet.
Design by Carnegie Orr

22 23

Typography
As design concerned with the conveyance of information,
the design of letterheads is a fundamentally typographic
exercise, and one in which the real thought begins after
the selection of an appropriate typeface. At its most
basic, the job entails sorting information into hierarchies
according to the way in which they will be used. For that
purpose, Jan Tschichold recommended asymmetrical
layouts. Herbert Spencer concurred: 'Asymmetrical
layout is flexible. It allows a precise and delicate control
of space in which emphasis is achieved by disposition
rather than by weight or size.'

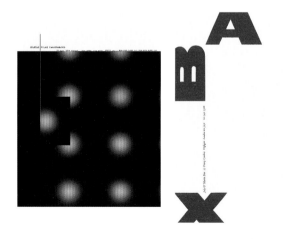

Letterhead for Celcius Films
with the address printed on the
reverse of the sheet. Design by
Carlos Segura of Segura Inc.

Letterhead for Martin Bax, the
editor of a poetry journal. Designed
by Alan Kitching of the Typography
Workshop and printed letterpress

In 'The New Typography', Tschichold described the component parts of the DIN standard letterhead: the recipient's address on the left (as once it has served its original purpose, it does not need to be seen in a filing system); space for receipt and treatment marks on the right; the four main pieces of information – your ref., your letter of, our ref. and the date – in one horizontal line under the headings; the firm's particulars; a left side margin of at least twenty millimetres. He also made the point that a single letter is part of a multiplicity – a correspondence – and that 'without order, such a multiplicity becomes unmanageable'.

While other designers have chosen to group information differently, or even to dispense with convention altogether, the basics hold true: essentially the design must strike a balance between effective communication and looking good. Writing in 'The New Typography', Jan Tschichold included an aside which, when one reads between the lines, sums up everything the approach to designing letterheads today should be: 'In general, the typography of the old letterheads took no notice of the fact that the letter as received should be written, signed and folded. Only when it is a completed whole can it look beautiful!'

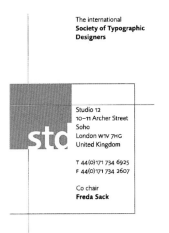

The international
Society of Typographic Designers

std

Studio 12
10–11 Archer Street
Soho
London W1V 7HG
United Kingdom

T 44(0)171 734 6925
F 44(0)171 734 2607

Co chair
Freda Sack

Postcard and business card for
Alice Twemlow, a writer, curator
and lecturer specialising in visual
communication. As most of
Twemlow's communications are
through phone, fax or e-mail, she
does not require a complete
stationery system in the traditional
sense. Design by Martin Perrin

The future
Writing in Berlin in 1926, the artist and designer El Lissitzky
foretold the death of letter writing. 'Correspondence
grows, the number of letters increased, the amount of
paper written on and materials used up swells, the
telephone call relieves the strain. Then comes further
growth of the communication network...then radio eases
the burden. The amount of material used is decreasing.'
Well, neither the telegraph, nor the radio, nor the
telephone, nor the fax has ever completely obviated the
need for letterheads – probably thanks to its unique
characteristics, as described earlier.

MESSAGE>>

ALICE TWEMLOW
VISUAL CULTURE
TEL/FAX : +212 206 0236
ADDRESS : 11 ABINGDON SQUARE 2F
          NEW YORK NEW YORK 10014
E-MAIL : TWEMLOW@AOL.COM
UK   : TEL/FAX +[0]1491 638591

ALICE TWEMLOW
VISUAL CULTURE
TEL/FAX : +212 206 0236
ADDRESS : 11 ABINGDON SQUARE 2F
          NEW YORK NEW YORK 10014
E-MAIL : TWEMLOW@AOL.COM
UK   : TEL/FAX +[0]1491 638591

Sketch of Parasite, an experimental
e-mail interface. Designed by US
design group io360

However, the booming volume of personal communications in the digital age will inevitably, in time, pose a new set of problems for the designer. In a world where global markets mean that face-to-face meetings are increasingly replaced by video conferences, what will take the place of the exchange of business cards? New York's Duffy Design, for one, has recently produced an interactive business card for itself. As the Web continues to grow at an exponential rate – and already it has grown from fewer than 300 computers on-line world-wide in 1981 to over 90 million in 1997 – more and more commercial transactions will be made between individuals at their PCs and a Web site.

Furthermore, as e-mail continues to gain ground on paper memos internally and letters externally, its users may want to transfer some of the sophistication of the letterhead to that new medium. US-based design group io360, for example, is among the pioneers in beginning to consider the future of the e-mail interface, in terms of matching style and structure with content (see below).

The present
So that's the past, and that's the future. The rest of this book is concerned with the present. This book is not intended to be an instruction manual; nor is it a history, or an awards annual. But in the following pages there are a wide variety of stationery systems designed by some of the best designers currently in practice, which I hope will inspire readers to look again at the letterhead, and re-evaluate its potential for good design. Whether they are rigid Swiss-schoolers or free-form deconstructionists, the common denominators between the designers of all of the stationery systems shown here are an eye for detail, a painstaking care with the raw materials of design and a wealth of original ideas.

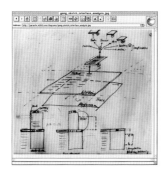

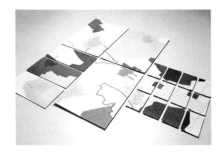 

26–51
Shape/Size/Fold

35 Little Russell Street
London WC1A 2HH

Telephone

+44 [0]171 637 1231

+44 [0]171 636 5015

Facsimile

+44 [0]171 631 3269

Client
Kinos Aarou

Design company
Wild & Frey

Brief
In a world driven by the profit motive, the
Zürich cinema Kinos Aarou is an outsider. It
selects what films it will show on the basis of
depth and cinematic quality rather than high
box office takes or explosive content. As a
result it shows a diverse mix of mainstream
Hollywood blockbuster movies, classics, art
house films, ciné noir and anything else that
makes the grade. When it commissioned Wild
& Frey to create a logo and stationery, the
cinema emphasised that the design should
reflect its stance on quality, distinguishing it
through simplicity and sophistication from the
run-of-the-mill cinema.

Kinocenter Ideal & Schloss
Kasinostr. 13, 5000 Aarau
T 062 822 40 82 F 824 29 71

Solution

The logo designed by Wild & Frey is, in itself, deceptively simple in appearance and can be reproduced easily and cheaply on tickets or posters. Being black and white it can even be photocopied without losing impact. In the logo, the letters of the name Kinos Aarou – of which, luckily, there are an equal number in each word – form the spool holes at the side of a reel of film, suggesting at a glance the nature of the business.

For the letterhead, the designers sourced oversized sheets of paper which were cut down by the printer, Digital Print, to leave a tab protruding from the top centre of what was now an A4 sheet. By sourcing the oversized sheets rather than just cutting the shape from a sheet of A3 paper, the designers reduced paper wastage and minimised costs. The logo was applied by printing the tab black and removing the letters of the cinema's name from its sides with very precise die-cuts.

The cuts are not straightforward and the scale on which the letters were reproduced was so small that the design took the printers to the limits of what is technically possible. To increase the chances of success, Wild & Frey gave the job to a specialist printer. When a letter is sent, the tab is folded over the sheet, casting a shadow where the light hits it.

Client
Casson Mann

Design company
Bell

Brief
Richard Mann and Dinah Casson are the two
partners in the interior design firm Casson
Mann. The pair have been in partnership for
ten years, using stationery designed by Mann,
but when the company recently started to win
big commissions from clients such as London's
Victoria & Albert Museum and Science
Museum, they decided to have the stationery
redesigned to reflect their changing status.
The pair were also keen to maintain a friendly,
if professional appearance, and Mann specified
that the letterhead should be able to work in
both portrait and landscape formats to enable
him to sketch on it.

Casson Mann Designers
4 Northington Street London WC1N 2JG

DINAH**CASSON**NNAM

T 0171 242 1112 F 0171 242 1113

Solution

Bell's solution is a letterhead that works both upside down, right way up and sideways. The names Casson and Mann share the letter 'N' at their ends, which was emboldened by designer Nick Bell to suggest collaboration and the complementary nature of the working partnership. As the type is arranged vertically rather than horizontally, the letterhead can be used either right way up, with the address in the bottom left-hand corner, or upside down, with the address in the top right-hand corner.

The fact that it is ranged up the sides of the sheet, with a continuous line of text saying 'Casson Mann' also running up the right-hand side of the sheet, allows the letterhead to be used in a landscape format without looking unnatural. That continuous line of text also acts as a column divider, allowing the letterhead to be used as an invoice. On the business cards, the names of Casson and Mann also share a letter, and the pair's Christian names are picked out in a lighter shade of grey to suggest friendliness and the personal touch.

Casson Mann Designers
4 Northington Street London WC1N 2JG

ROGER**MAN**N OSS∀Ɔ

T 0171 242 1112 F 0171 242 1113

CASSO**NN**AM

Casson Mann Designers
4 Northington Street London WC1N 2JG
T 0171 242 1112
F 0171 242 1113

Dinah Casson Roger Mann

Casson **Mann** Limited   Company Registration no. 3201095, England & Wales
Registered Office: 1 Printing House Yard London E2 7PR VAT no. 448 0176 79

MANNOSS∀Ɔ

Client
Nick Turner

Design company
Alan Dye

Brief
Nick Turner is the in-house photographer at the
London-based design consultancy Pentagram.
When he wanted a stationery system, he asked
Pentagram designer Alan Dye, who has since
left the company, to work on the project.
Simplicity was the order of the day, with Turner
requiring only a business card and letterhead
which he wanted to look restrained and
graphically simple.

Nick Turner Photographer
13 Tanners Hill
Deptford London SE8 4PJ
T 0181 691 9044
M 0973 339659

Solution
Alan Dye followed Turner's instructions almost to the letter, using no illustration and setting the type, printed in red and black inks, in American Typewriter. However, he couldn't resist making a reference to the nature of Turner's business using a subtle die-cut at the edge of both letterhead and business card. The unusual shape is taken from the crop on the edge of a 5 x 4 transparency, a shape familiar to anyone who deals with photography and photographers on a regular basis.

The shape was reproduced at actual size so Dye was able to supply the printer, Loughlin Print, with an actual transparency as artwork. The off-white paper stock was selected for its classic look and feel, but Dye had to make sure that it was heavy enough to support a die-cut without losing its edge.

Client
Sutherland Building Services

Design company
HGV

Brief
HGV partner Jim Sutherland's brother runs a small building company and asked HGV to design him a letterhead and business card. His requirements were that while the job should not be too expensive, it should allow him to stand out from the competition.

62b Saltoun Road
London SW2 1ER
Telephone 071 738 6751
Mobile 0831 817 208

Solution

Literal stand-out was the chosen route as Jim Sutherland wanted to include an element of three-dimensionality in the letterhead and business card as a reference to the building trade. This was achieved through the use of two simple die-cuts on the first fold line of the letterhead which, when the scored and folded letter is opened, produce a red house brick on the right-hand side of the sheet.

Because the technical requirements of the job were not great – the colours and die-cuts were comparatively simple – the printing could be done by a basic printer, making the letterhead affordable to a small company.

Client
Celcius Films

Design company
Segura Inc.

Brief
New York-based film production company
Celcius films commissioned Segura Inc.
to design a stationery system that was both
graphically impactful and at the same time
modern and clean.

Solution

In reconciling the two demands, Segura Inc. 'broke the rules' of letterhead design. Having decided to consider the sheet as a whole as a canvas, the designer Carlos Segura chose to put the address and other typographic elements on the reverse. The nature of the company's business was referenced through illustrations of glowing circles of light, suggesting the lights of film studios.

Further reference to the industry was made through the use of die-cuts at each corner of the letterhead as Segura felt that the rounded edges would be reminiscent of an aesthetic associated with Hollywood glamour of the 1940s and '50s.

CELSIUS FILMS INCORPORATED.

37 east 18th street
new york, new york. 10003 usa

212.253.7400 (t) 212.253.8199 (f)

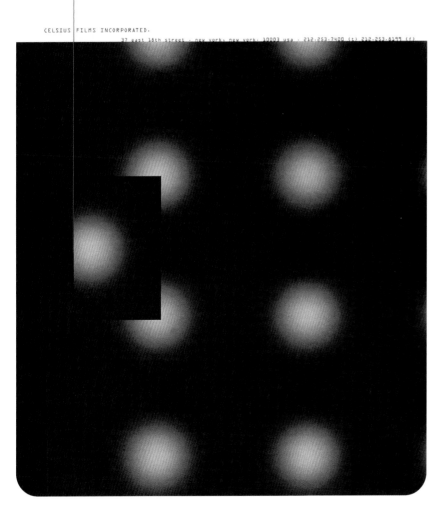

CELSIUS FILMS INCORPORATED.
37 east 18th street · new york, new york. 10003 usa · 212.253.7400 (t) 212.253.8199 (f)

Client
Upside Down

Design company
Intro

Brief
Seeing things from a different perspective is
the unique selling point of Edmundo, a film-
maker whose work is mainly in the area of TV
commercials. As a Spaniard working in
London, and a leading creative independent in
his own right, Edmundo wanted his stationery
to reflect the fact that his company, Upside
Down, stands apart from the herd, striving to
be different and original. Due to the nature of
the industry in which he and the advertising
agencies who form the bulk of his clients work,
the letterhead also had to be fun, eye-catching,
and creatively inspired.

Solution
Rendering the company's name graphically,
Intro printed the name and contact details
literally upside down, at the bottom of the sheet,
so that they can be read only when the sheet
is turned so that the typewritten letter itself is
now upside down. A hint of Edmundo's own
personality comes across in a collection of
four photographs of the film-maker himself, also
printed upside down, demonstrating how to
view the letterhead from 'a different perspective'.

59

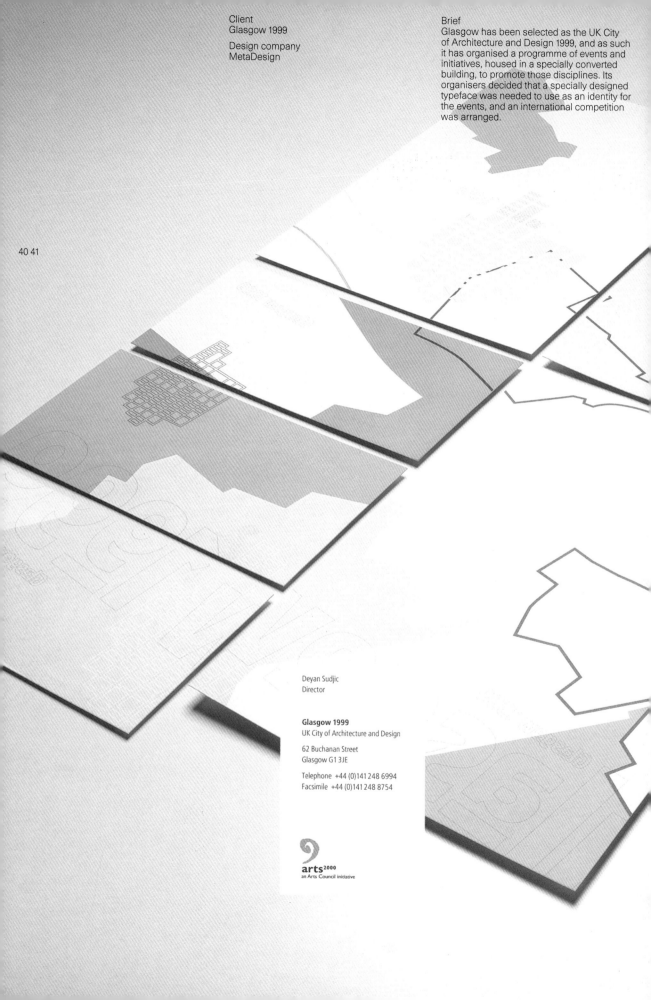

Client
Glasgow 1999

Design company
MetaDesign

Brief
Glasgow has been selected as the UK City of Architecture and Design 1999, and as such it has organised a programme of events and initiatives, housed in a specially converted building, to promote those disciplines. Its organisers decided that a specially designed typeface was needed to use as an identity for the events, and an international competition was arranged.

Deyan Sudjic
Director

Glasgow 1999
UK City of Architecture and Design

62 Buchanan Street
Glasgow G1 3JE

Telephone +44 (0)141 248 6994
Facsimile +44 (0)141 248 8754

arts²⁰⁰⁰
an Arts Council initiative

This was won by MetaDesign London, which was then asked to create a logo as well as a complete typeface. Before these were complete, however, Glasgow 1999's organisers realised that they needed a range of stationery for promotional purposes.

Solution
In the absence of a completed logo or typeface, MetaDesign had to find an alternative way of identifying the programme and representing the city. A city map was abstracted by dividing and colouring it along the lines of its postal districts and applied to the reverse of a sheet of A2 paper.

From this, two letterheads, one continuation sheet, and three compliments slips are cut, each carrying on its back a further abstracted fragment of the city map, which became a sort of interim identity.

Client
Silk Purse

Design company
The Partners

Brief
When the architectural practice Plinke Leaman
& Browning discovered that no software
program existed that fitted the particular
requirements of architects in monitoring costs
and planning the use of resources, it designed
its own, named it Prophet, tested it and then
set about marketing it to other architects.
Reckoning that computer software was a rather
dry and boring product, PLB wanted to inject
an elements of wit into the identity of the new
business, which after an internal competition,
was named The Silk Purse Company.

The Silk Purse Company
Christopher Higgins ARICS
The Silk Purse Company Ltd
5 The Square Winchester SO23 9ES
Tel: Winchester (0962) 63603

The Silk Purse Company
5 The Square Winchester S
Tel: Winchester (0962) 63603
Registered in England No 201960
VAT Registration No 411 9532 71
Directors
Nigel Charlesworth DipArch
Stephen Alsford BSc MTech
Christopher Higgins ARICS
Clive Houghton MCIOB

Solution
The name Silk Purse refers to the old expression 'making a silk purse out of a sow's ear' – taking something ordinary and turning it into something extraordinary. Design company The Partners took this as its cue for the identity, and referenced the expression through the use of a fold in the top right-hand corners of the letterhead, compliments slip and business card.

Only the area designed to be folded is printed in pink on the reverse of the sheet, which, when a simple snout-like graphic is added, makes the overall effect decidedly piggy. Through adopting a minimalist approach, the designers hoped to ensure that their clients would not be mistaken for butchers, and that recipients would be sufficiently charmed by the wit in the design to remember the company name while overlooking the more tedious aspects of the product.

The Silk Purse Company

Client
Tim Flach

Design company
Roundel

Brief
Tim Flach is a London-based photographer
best known for his work with subjects from the
natural world. When he commissioned Roundel
to design his stationery, he was keen that the
letterhead, compliments slip and business card
should reflect not only the subjects with which
he works, but also communicate that he uses
a variety of unusual photographic techniques.
It was also important that the stationery would
act as much as a promotional device as a
communications tool.

Tim Flach Photography   Tim Flach   17 Willow Street London EC2A 4QH   T: 0171 613 1894   F: 0171 613 5802   Mobile: 0836 372 641

Date

Solution
Roundel illustrated the stationery with a series
of Flach's blue-tinted 'photograms' of the natural
world, fulfiling the brief's requirements that the
stationery should reference his technique-based
work and his subject matter. The letterhead
and compliments slip were made unique and
particularly distinctive, however, by the decision
to produce them in the same sizes as
photographic paper: the letterhead, for example,
is ten by eight inches, a standard photographic
measurement, and works in a landscape format.
This clever touch not only references Flach's
business – photography – but also makes the
letterhead memorable and distinctive.

Tim Flach   17 Willow Street London EC2A 4QH   **T:** 0171 613 1894   **F:** 0171 613 5802   **Mobile:** 0836 372 641

Tim Flach Photography

Tim Flach   17 Willow Street London EC2A 4QH   **T:** 0171 613 1894   **F:** 0171 613 5802   **Mobile:** 0836 372 641

Date

with compliments

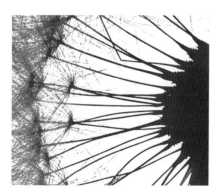

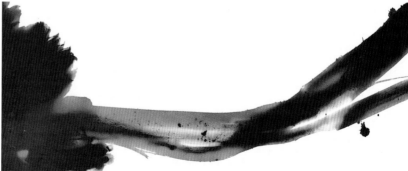

Brief
Celia Keyworth runs a catering company that prides itself on the quality of its food and the friendliness of its staff. The waiters and waitresses, who are mostly out-of-work actors and actresses, give the company a slightly Bohemian air, unlike some of Keyworth's more formal competitors, and she was keen to have these qualities reflected in her stationery.

Vat No. 421 6627 68

Solution
To suggest the deliciousness of the food and
inject a note of levity into the material,
Pentagram partner John Rushworth created a
bite-mark logo that was applied to letterheads,
business cards, brochures, moving cards,
folders and any other Celia Keyworth
communication through the use of a die-cut.
The stationery has been redesigned since
the mark was first introduced, but the die-cut
in the top corner has remained.

Celia Keyworth's Food
108 Torriano Avenue
London NW5 2SD
Telephone 071 267 8872
Fax 071 482 1426

Celia Keyworth

Celia Keyworth's Food
108 Torriano Avenue
London NW5 2SD
Telephone 071 267 8872
Fax 071 482 1426

Client
Intro

Design company
Intro

Brief
Design company Intro felt that the way it was
perceived within the industry and by potential
clients did not fully do justice to its abilities.
The company was well known for its work in
the music and youth-oriented sectors, but felt
that potential clients in the corporate sector
might be put off by this image. However, while
Intro wished to convince a new breed of client
that it was available for corporate work, it had
to avoid alienating its existing clients or
diminishing the strong reputation it had built in
that area.

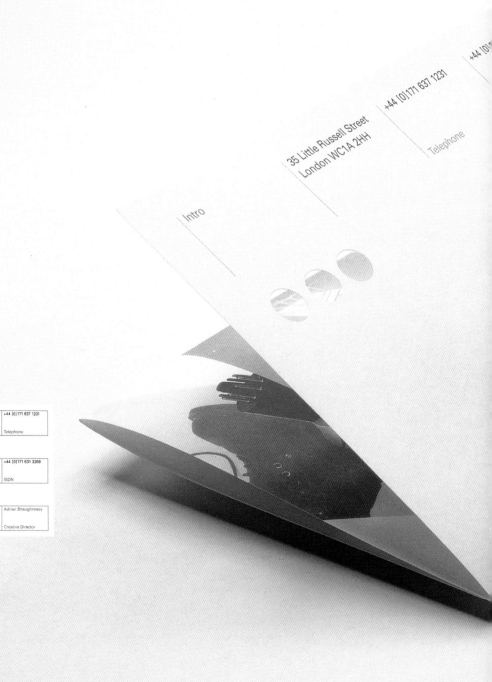

35 Little Russell Street
London WC1A 2HH

+44 (0)171 637 1231

Telephone

Intro

Intro	35 Little Russell Street London WC1A 2HH	+44 (0)171 637 1231
		Telephone
0973 221688	+44 (0)171 636 5015	+44 (0)171 631 3269
Mobile	Facsimile	ISDN
as@intro.demon.co.uk		Adrian Shaughnessy
Email		Creative Director

Solution
Intro's solution was to create several different letterheads around a flexible logo that was designed and introduced at the same time as the stationery redesign. The mark – three coloured dots – was essentially corporate in appearance, but could be applied to the stationery in a number of ways. Printed straight onto the sheet, the three dots and the clean, Swiss-influenced typography that is another of the company's hallmarks add up to a letterhead that might be sent to a bank or corporate client.

The letterhead shown here, however, retains some of the playfulness and fresh, quirky originality for which the company is known. The letterhead uses three die-cuts which, when the sheet is folded, expose the three colours of the logo from three images printed on the reverse of the sheet. In this way the corporate look is subverted in a way calculated to appeal to Intro's clients in the creative and youth-oriented industries.

Client
Sandringham School Stamp Club

Design company
Billy Mawhinney

Brief
Sandringham School in St. Albans, England, is a government-funded school taking pupils from the age of eleven until eighteen. The commitment of its teachers has made it a great success story, to the extent that its head teacher has been appointed to a government advisory body. Parents are actively encouraged to help the school in any way that they can, and those working in fields such as advertising and design are occasionally asked to provide design and promotional work for the school.

The Sandringham School Stamp Club wanted a printed letterhead of its own for communication with members, but could not afford the paper and print costs. A solution was found by parent Billy Mawhinney, who was at the time creative director of advertising agency J. Walter Thompson.

Solution
Mawhinney recognised that, as the Club could afford neither expensive paper stock nor printing, a letterhead was needed which used neither. The paper is recycled A4 manila envelopes, while the postmark logo at the top of the sheet is applied with a rubber stamp, made to order by Mawhinney, of a type which can be bought cheaply at stationery stores. The effect is completed by the addition of a one penny stamp. The result is an appropriate, impactful letterhead that comes within the budget even of a school stamp club.

Partners
Justin Buckingham
Katharine Scott

Studio
71 Lambeth Walk
London
SE11 6DX

52–77
Materials

ARTOMATIC

65 Stirling Road
London W3 8DJ
T   0181 896 6666
F   0181 896 6611
  ON 0181 896 6622
        artomatic.co.uk

ANNI KUAN

Client
Rollmann

Design company
Birgit Eggers

Brief
Lies Rollmann is a freelance architect working
in the Netherlands. Her style is simple, which
belies the fact that she is interested in using
unusual materials in her work. As a sole
practitioner, working for a wide variety of clients,
her stationery system had to reflect those
characteristics, as well as being flexible and
relatively inexpensive. It also had to reflect the
qualities of her own work – 'designed' without
being fussy, practical and yet stylish.

54 55

Solution
Designer Birgit Eggers chose to base the
system on simple, informative adhesive
stickers. The advantages of this are twofold.
First, the stickers can be used for business
cards, letterheads, architectural plans,
sketchbooks and so on, saving the expense of
printing all of those items individually. Second,
the stickers can themselves be attached to
materials that would otherwise prove difficult to
print on.

The diversity of materials used in Rollmann's
architectural work can therefore be reflected
in those used in her communications. Eggers
sourced and supplied materials as diverse as
lightweight, translucent sheets of tracing paper
and a black compliments card covered in a
fine web of cotton thread. Because of the
flexibility of the sticker system, Rollmann can
add to the range of materials in the future if
she chooses, or even create bespoke cards
or letters for particular jobs.

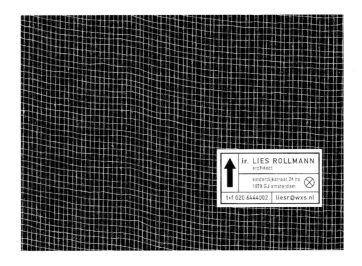

Client
Kid Marketing Group

Design company
Segura Inc.

Brief
As consumers become ever more fragmented in their consumption habits, and ever more advertising aware, agencies find ever more sophisticated ways of targeting them. The Kid Marketing Group, based in Chicago, is a division of the advertising agency DDB Needham Worldwide, set up specifically to market products to children. Although the letters and business cards would have an adult audience, when the agency commissioned Segura Inc. to design its stationery, it requested that the stationery should look like it was intended for children, with a playful, colourful tone.

Kid Marketing Group

DDB Needham Worldwide

303 East Wacker Drive, Chicago, Illinois 60601-5282   tel. 312·861·0200   fax. 312·552·2383

Solution

Segura Inc. devised a logo for the Group that appears to be hand-drawn with a crayon, and added other touches to the stationery reminiscent of the paraphernalia of childhood: the reverse of the sheet is covered by a typographic illustration saying things like 'cereal' and 'toys', for example, and there are spaces on the back of a business card in which its owner can fill their own name, address, job title and so on, in the manner of children's school books.

The effect was completed by the choice of paper stock – a recycled, uncoated stock containing coloured speckles within the sheet. The colours flecking the paper echo those in the logo and contribute to the overall sense of childish colourfulness and gaiety.

DDB Needham Worldwide

Kid Marketing Group

303 East Wacker Drive, Chicago, Illinois 60601-5282
tel. 312-861-0200 fax 312-552-2383

Client
Artomatic

Design company
Artomatic

Brief
Artomatic is a creatively driven printing
company, but when it comes to producing its
own stationery, the printers are not so much
concerned with showing what they can do, as
doing what they like. The company's identity
was originally designed by the influential
graphic designer Malcolm Garrett, and he
continues to work with the company on an
informal basis whenever updates are required,
but the choice of materials is left in the hands
of those whose business it is to know what
they are capable of – the printers themselves.

Solution
As Artomatic began as a screen-printing company, its letterheads were traditionally screen-printed. However, when the company grew to a point where screen-printing was no longer feasible, the printers aimed to achieve a similar effect by using a holographic foil over which the company logo was litho printed. As holographic foils are susceptible to damage in the heat of desktop laser printers, the decision to use a foil necessitated testing many different papers to find one with sufficient substance and tooth to hold the foil and withstand the rigours of laser printing.

Most of the firm's business cards are made from stiff brown card, but a chance connection with a client opened up a source of one material with irresistible qualities, leading to a second run of cards: at one point in its growth, Artomatic took over a smaller firm of printers, G & B Arts, one of whose clients was Formula One motor racing team McLaren, through whom Artomatic was able to source the carbon fibre – the substance from which racing cars are built – for its business cards.

Carbon fibre is the most shatterproof material in the world, making it difficult for recipients of the card to simply scrumple it up and bin it. An added advantage is that the cards, like the letterhead, enhance Artomatic's reputation for creatively led printing on strange materials using unusual processes.

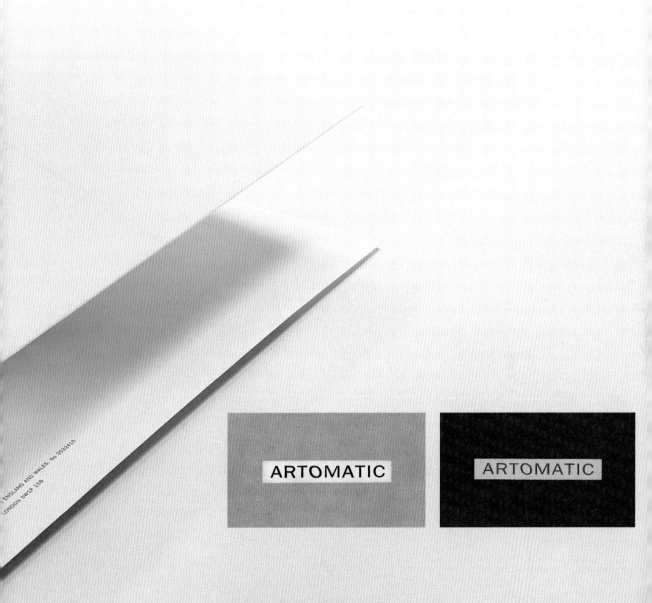

Client
On Stage

Design company
Area

Brief
While it does not design clothes itself, German fashion boutique On Stage sells clothes by top designers from all over the world. When it commissioned London-based graphic design company Area to create its stationery, the brief asked for a sense of sharpness and sophistication.

Solution

The project began with the creation of a logo. The 'O' of On Stage was turned into a globe, suggesting the company's global supply network. Locations on the world map were picked out in foil blocks, as was the name itself, to lend an air of modern sophistication to the design. In accordance with German legal requirements, information such as the company's banking details are included on the letterhead, alongside its address, arranged down the right-hand side of the sheet. Area used both serif (Didot) and sans serif (Futura) typefaces to suggest modernity with respectability.

The director of On Stage had asked that he be given his own letterhead in order to distinguish his communications from those of others in the company. This was achieved through printing the director's letterhead on tracing paper while the standard letterhead is on a plain white uncoated stock, thus introducing a hierarchy of importance through the use of materials.

Franco Bruccoleri

Fashion Stage
Franco Bruccoleri GmbH
Zeppelinstraße 47
81669 München
Telefon
+49 (0)89 48 06 01/0
Telefax
+49 (0)89 48 06 01 40

Showroom
Lindemannstraße 37
40237 Düsseldorf
Telefon
+49 (0)211 68 11 90
Telefax
+49 (0)211 679 82 12

Client
Esprit Europe

Design company
HGV

Brief
Esprit Europe is a parcel delivery service and a subsidiary of Eurostar, the company that operates trains running through the Channel Tunnel between England and France. The company was being launched into a crowded marketplace populated by household names – its competitors are well-established international express delivery firms such as FedEx, DHL and TNT, each of which has been operating in the market with great success for many years. Esprit Europe realised from the outset that it could not afford to match the advertising spend of those companies and therefore decided not to try. Instead, it opted to concentrate its marketing spend on the creation of a strong graphic identity, including a stationery system.

Solution

As well as a logo suggesting a speeding parcel in the shape of a Eurostar train, HGV gave the company an aesthetic based on the graphic ephemera of the couriering business – delivery vans, for example, look like a parcel with a brown livery, and an address label and 'Urgent' sticker on the side. The letterhead itself uses a brown packaging paper called Paperback Craft to reinforce in the mind of the recipient what sector the company operates in.

The use of brown paper and card, not only on the stationery range but also in brochures, direct mail and so on, has given the company as strong and recognisable an identity as it could have hoped to achieve through a vastly more expensive television advertising campaign – the marketing route preferred by many of its competitors.

Client
Anni Kuan

Design company
Sagmeister Inc.

Two worlds collide in the collection of fashion
designer Anni Kuan. Her clothes are essentially
Western but with a strong Eastern influence.
They are simple in style with playful touches.
It was the nature of the collection itself that
provided the brief when Kuan commissioned
Sagmeister Inc. to design her stationery.

Solution
Designer Stefan Sagmeister looked for a way to express the Eastern influence on Kuan's clothes without resorting to clichés such as the use of Chinese characters. Instead, the meeting of two cultures is represented typographically through splitting the letters of the name Anni Kuan into their vertical and horizontal components. On the business card, for example, the name is revealed when the card is folded and die-cuts between the vertical lines on its front face expose the horizontals and diagonals printed on the inside of the card, spelling the name.

A similar effect is created by the letterhead when it is folded and placed inside an envelope. Sagmeister created a bespoke translucent vellum envelope, onto which were printed the vertical components of the logo. When the letter is folded – it is a relatively complicated and unusual fold – and placed inside, the horizontal components line up with the verticals to complete the name. Besides allowing Sagmeister to 'build' the logo in two stages, the choice of materials for the envelope also hints at the look of Kuan's own designs – many of her dresses are comprised of a sheer wrap over an opaque base layer.

ANNI KUAN

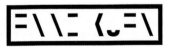

242 W 38TH ST NEW YORK NY 10018 PHONE 212 704 4038 FAX 704 0651

Client
Glasshammer

Design company
HDR Design

Brief
Having created the ironic name 'Glasshammer'
in conjunction with HDR Design, this model-
making company asked its designers to create
a logo and stationery system. Glasshammer's
clients are advertising agencies and the
stationery had to appeal to them, but not in
a way that was artificial. The company also
requested that the stationery should have an
element of 'special effects' about it, but that
it should still look sober and professional,
reflecting not only the seriousness with which
the model makers approach their work, but
also the precision involved in their craft.

Vat Reg Number
626 1915 42

Solution
A balance was struck by combining typographic
clarity with an unusual paper stock. The
transluccncy of the Simulator paper references
the 'glass' in the company's name, and also
allows its new logo, a hammer overlaid on a
letter 'G', to stand out. The compliments slips
were made out of the same paper, while the
business cards are made out of tracing paper.
An element of designer/client interactivity
was introduced into the design process as
Glasshammer's employees were invited to
choose a crop of the hammer and 'G' logo to
illustrate their own business card.

Partners
Justin Buckingham
Katharine Scott

Glasshammer

Studio
71 Lambeth Walk
London
SE11 6DX

Phone/Fax
071 582 5802

Client
Rachel Eager

Design company
Werner Design Works

Brief
As a young copywriter, fresh out of college,
Rachel Eager needed stationery more to attract
and develop new relationships with potential
clients than to communicate with existing ones.
She decided that she would like to target
design companies and advertising agencies
looking for someone with a sense fun rather
than a more corporate approach, and briefed
Werner Design Works to create a stationery
system that would reflect this.

After a consultation with the designers, it was also decided that Eager, who had only recently graduated from college, should adopt an honest approach in her pitches, and not pretend through her stationery to be more established and experienced than she was. Budgetary constraints also meant that while she wanted a distinctive, entertaining stationery system, it had to be inexpensive.

Solution
Developing a school theme, and hinting playfully at the fact that Eager was a recent graduate, lined paper was sourced at low cost from a school supplies shop. To save the cost of printing the sheets, a range of stickers carrying Eager's contact details was created. These could be affixed not only to the letterhead itself but also to other communications such as parcels or invoices.

A set of folders or pockets, sourced at auction from a bankrupt printer, was also added to the stationery system. In the US these have a particular resonance as examination papers and school reports are usually submitted in this way. The business cards were printed on Beveridge Placard Board which, because Eager only required a small number of cards, the designers were able to get for free as samples.

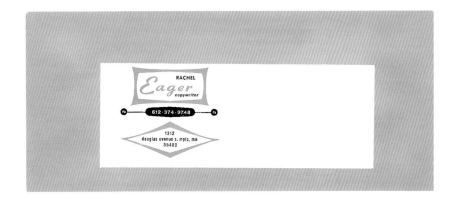

Client
Ursula Wild

Design company
Wild & Frey

Brief
As the sister of Heinz Wild, a partner in design
company Wild & Frey, Ursula Wild did not have
to look far when she wanted someone to
design a range of stationery for her business.
Ursula Wild is a specialist in foot massage and
related relaxation techniques based in Zürich,
Switzerland. The service is very personal and
the individual client is important and well taken
care of. It was important that
the stationery should communicate this with
a feel that captured both the personal and the
medical professional aspects of the business.

The specific stationery items she requested were a letterhead, business card, envelope and appointments card, but it was stressed that the system should be flexible enough to allow for future additions – she has recently started selling her own treatments in bottles, for example.

Solution
The designers built flexibility into the stationery by using stickers. These had to precisely match the colour of the letterhead and business card, to which they would be attached, and so Wild & Frey sourced an appropriate stock for both the stickers and the stationery items themselves from German paper maker Gmünd, and asked the printers, Digital Print, to give the stickers an adhesive backing. The paper, which is slightly rough with a hand-finished feel, suggested the purity and precision of a medical process through its clean, white appearance, but this was complemented by its warmer, more natural texture, which gives it the personal feel demanded by the brief.

Another 'personal' touch is found on the business card, which, when given to important customers can be tied with string. The time involved in preparing the card suggests that it is precious, and that its recipient is important to Ursula Wild, promoting good client relations.

Client
Photonica

Design company
Frost Design

Brief
When the big Japanese photolibrary Photonica
opened a headquarters for its European
operations in London, it commissioned Frost
Design to create a range of stationery
materials as part of a new identity which was
to play a significant part in announcing the
library's presence as an autonomously
operating UK office.

72 73

Amana Italy S.r.l. Via Borgonuovo, 5. 20121 Milano, Italia Telefono 02 86996001 Fax 02 86999079

photonica

Partita IVA 123 3082057

Solution

Frost Design took the decision not to use any of the photolibrary's images in either the logo, which in the end was a typographic solution, or the stationery, even though the library's images are highly distinctive. Instead, Photonica's Japanese origins were suggested through the use of type and materials: the name Photonica is written vertically down the right-hand side of the page, in the style of Japanese script. Meta was selected as Photonica's corporate typeface. Japanese associations were also made through the choice of paper for the project: a recycled stock – Paperback Metaphor – was picked for the letterhead.

The paper was selected for its rough, grainy texture, which the designers felt was reminiscent of Japanese paper and packaging materials. For each subsequent piece of material designed for the library, Frost Design has sourced an unusual and interesting paper type, and used a range of finishing techniques such as embossing and debossing, to give it the requisite Japanese feel. As a result, the tactility and texture of the materials has, in a sense, become a trademark of Photonica in Europe.

Amana Italy
Via Borgonuovo, 5. 20121 Milano
Tel. 02 86996001
Fax. 02 86990979

Client
Koji Tatsuno

Design company
Area

Brief
Fashion designer Koji Tatsuno is an inveterate globe trotter. Originally from Japan, he now works from Paris but it was when he was based in London with a satellite showroom in Milan that he asked Area to design his stationery. Tatsuno's clothes are characterised by unusual fabrics and a clever use of materials.

KOJI TATSUNO

UKON ITALIA SRL Via Spartaco 10, 20135 Milan, Italy. Tel. 02 5510989. Fax. 02 55180364.

Cod Fisc e P IVA 08891440151, CCIAA 1255059, Trib Milan 274067/7063/17 Cap Soc 20.000.000.

Solution
It was Tatsuno's treatment of materials that gave Area designer Richard Smith his cue in creating the letterhead. Smith selected a lightweight stock – 90 gsm Ingersley Poster Paper – which comes printed red on the face of the sheet. Smith turned the sheet around so that its reverse became its face. Because the stock is very thin, some of the red ink from the side which would normally be printed on (the red side) seeps through to the reverse face – the side on which Tatsuno will write his letters.

Although the side that the letters will be written on is one which wouldn't ordinarily be seen, it has the positive quality of being unique – each sheet is different, and therefore suggestive of quality and expense. The tactility of the stock, which has a rough but fragile feel, also references the fabrics used in Tatsuno's work.

KOJI TATSUNO

UKON ITALIA SRL Via Spartaco 10, 20135 Milan, Italy.
Tel, 02 5510989. Fax, 02 55180364.

Client
Azone & Associates

Design company
Azone & Associates

Brief
The best-known example is origami, but in
general the Japanese are well-known around
the world for their creative use of paper. When
Tokyo-based design group Azone & Associates
redesigned its own stationery, great care was
taken to choose a stock that met all of the
designers' requirements.

▶ Azone+Associates

Design consulting and more.

Solution

Despite being printed in both English and Japanese, the letterhead and business card are very simple in appearance, using a basic serif and only one colour of ink. The letterhead and card were both printed letterpress and it was one of the key requirements of the stock that it should both support the letterpress printing and bring out the colour of the ink. The designers were also determined to use a recycled stock out of consideration for the environment.

Although it is now possible to get recycled grades that are as smooth as any other stock, Azone & Associates wanted the paper to have a rough texture to make the experience of handling the letterhead a sensuous one. The paper selected, Gilesse, was one which met all of the specifications: furthermore, it has a subtle grid of squares running as a watermark through the paper which brings the sheet to life when it is held up to the light, and its off-white colour adds warmth and flavour to an otherwise austere piece of design.

Design consulting and more.

Phone: 03-5411-0336
Fax: 03-5411-0345

株式会社アゾーン アンド アソシエイツ
〒107 東京都港区南青山 3-16-1 メゾン巴 5F
3-16-1 Minami Aoyama 5F
Minato-ku, Tokyo 107 Japan

Haruki Mori ▶ Azone+Associates
Director / Designer

ディレクター / デザイナー　森 治樹

78–103
Typography

Client
Möhr

Design company
Odermatt & Tissi

Brief
Hans Möhr is, in general terms, a consultant on
cultural matters to government bodies as well
as large firms, but the actual nature of his work
is harder to define. When he commissioned
Odermatt & Tissi to create a stationery system
he explained that while he wanted something
simple in appearance, it should also set him
apart from other consultants working in the
same field.

Alpenstrasse 31
Postfach
CH-8801 Thalwil
Telefon 01 772 35 35
Fax 01 772 35 36
E-mail
moehr.cmc@bluewin.ch

Solution

Because the diverse and imprecise nature of the services Möhr provides would have been difficult to illustrate, and because the brief called for a simple appearance, designer Rosmarie Tissi opted for a typographic solution. Setting the 'M' initial and the umlaut which sits above the letter 'o' in Möhr's name in Gill, Tissi turned the characters into the cornerstones of a structure. Three square dots were also added to the 'mark', against which the three strands of Möhr's business are described – communication, management and cultural consultancy.

The remainder of the text, set in Futura, is arranged in various positions around this mark on the envelope, business card, fax header, invoice and letterhead, but is omitted from the continuation sheet, which is identified only by the basic elements of the 'logo'.

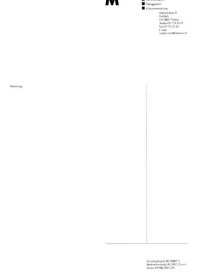

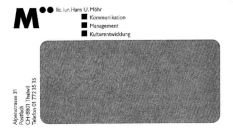

Client
Parameta

Design company
Pentagram

Brief
When Jon Greenfield left design company
Pentagram, where he had worked as an
associate, to set up his own architectural
practice, he asked his former colleague,
Pentagram partner David Hillman, to design
his stationery. Pentagram as a consultancy
is known for its graphic wit and fondness for
wordplay.

Solution
The name Greenfield had chosen for his practice – Parameta – immediately suggested a typographic solution: the word parameter actually has a precise meaning in mathematics, but it is commonly understood to mean a limit or furthest point.

Hillman opted to break the word parameta into four parts which he ranged around the four corners of the page, creating a visual joke in which the image of the word echoes its sense – Parameta is at the parameters of the page. The company's address, as well as the chunks of the word Parameta, were set in Franklin Gothic.

PARAMETA Architects
Cowcross Court
75-77 Cowcross Street
London EC1M 6BP
Tel +44 (0)171 250 33 32
Fax +44 (0)171 250 37 72
parameta97@aol.com

David Nixon
BA(Hons) RIBA FRSA
Jon Greenfield
BA(Hons) BArch RIBA

PA   RA

PARAMETA Architects
Cowcross Court
75-77 Cowcross Street
London EC1M 6BP
Tel +44 (0)171 250 33 32
Fax +44 (0)171 250 37 72
parameta97@aol.com

David Nixon
BA(Hons) RIBA FRSA

ME   TA

Client
Merens Architects

Design company
Birgit Eggers

Brief
As a freelance interior designer working alone,
Marina Merens needed a stationery system
that was flexible enough to cope with all of her
requirements: it had to be corporate-looking
enough to send to potential clients, while with
sufficient individual personality to emphasise
the personal touch offered to a client by a
freelance designer. In short, Merens was
selling herself, but did not want to look small-
scale and amateurish in comparison with
larger companies.

marina merens · utrechtsedwarsstraat 30b · 1017 WG Amsterdam · tel 020 427 9883 · fax 020 427 3305 · merens@compuserve.com

MERENS
interieurarchitect

Solution
Designer Birgit Eggers opted for a typographic solution, beginning by creating a logo to represent the nature of Merens' business: the components of the logo – two 'ones' facing one another and a colon in between – not only form an 'M', but also suggest 'one-to-one', a concept that itself has two meanings in the case of Merens. As a sole practitioner she works alone, and therefore enjoys a 'one-to-one' relationship with her clients, and furthermore, the ratio is a reference to the scales used in architects' plans, one-to-one, of course, being life-size.

Eggers wanted to keep the letterhead typographically clean to reflects Merens' own design style, and selected the austere News Gothic typeface for the address. The choice of transparent materials relates to the spatial nature of interior design, with a business card that can be used to literally encompass examples of the company's work, thus becoming itself a three-dimensional object.

Client
MetaDesign

Design company
MetaDesign

Brief
The international design consultancy
MetaDesign was founded by type designer
Erik Spiekermann in Germany. Its letterheads
today are based on original concepts by
Spiekermann and retain evidence of the
company's German roots in their use of
typography. MetaDesign as a whole believes
in functionality and simplicity in design and
this is reflected in the letterhead. The
company has offices in Berlin, London and
San Francisco, each of which has a letterhead
based on the guidelines originally set out by
Spiekermann. The example shown here is
from MetaDesign London.

MetaUnion
Design Limited
Registered in the UK
number 297-5311

Directors
Tim Fendley
Robin Richmond
Erik Spiekermann

Solution
The letterhead as a whole is considered as a piece of information design, and is typographically ordered according to the priority given to each piece of information. Beneath the surface lies an extremely complicated grid that all MetaDesign's communications are laid out on, but the surface effect is of simplicity and clarity.

Dotted arrows show, in a logical sequence, who the letter is from, who it is to, and so on, while the company address is placed in the bottom right-hand corner of the sheet as the information is of secondary importance to the letter itself and the information recorded by the arrows.

The arrows themselves, as well as the typeface in which letters are written, are set in Meta, the typeface designed by Erik Spiekermann. This typeface has the double advantage of being associated with the company, as well as being specifically designed for laser printing, and therefore working effectively on a letterhead. Red bars bleeding off the sides of the page add further functionality to the letterhead, allowing it to be identified within a filing system.

MetaDesign London
5–8 Hardwick Street
London EC1R 4RB
+44 (0)171 520 1000
Fax +44 (0)171 520 1099
mail@metadesign.co.uk

MetaDesign Berlin
Bergmannstraße 102
D–10961 Berlin
+49 30 695 79 200
Fax +49 30 695 79 222

MetaDesign San Francisco
350 Pacific Avenue
San Francisco CA 94111
+1 415 627 0790
Fax +1 415 627 0795

MetaDesign Virtual
www.metadesign.com

You are what you are seen to be

MetaDesign

→ **Robin Richmond**
Director

Rational Modernism – with character

↓
MetaDesign Berlin
Bergmannstraße 102
D–10961 Berlin
+49 30 695 79 200
Fax +49 30 695 79 222

MetaDesign San Francisco
350 Pacific Avenue
San Francisco CA 94111
+1 415 627 0790
Fax +1 415 627 0795

MetaDesign Virtual
www.metadesign.com

MetaDesign London
5–8 Hardwick Street
London EC1R 4RB

+44 (0)171 520 1000

Fax +44 (0)171 520 1099
robin@metadesign.co.uk

Client
John Rushworth

Design company
Alan Kitching

JOHN, SUE & MAXINE RUSHWORTH
WINCEL LODGE, TOMPSETS BANK,
FOREST ROW, EAST SUSSEX RH18 5LL
TELEPHONE 0342 82 4699

Solution
Free from the constraints of corporate design – the personal letters would be mostly hand-written rather than typed, for example – Kitching selected an unusual shape for the letterhead: the squared-off A4 sheet still fits into a standard DL envelope when folded in half, however. The initials of each member of Rushworth's family were positioned in each of the four corners of the letterhead. A continuation sheet was also created for each individual family member, identified through printing the initial in the same place as it sits on the letterhead itself.

In this way, the continuation sheet identifies the sender of the letter as an individual. The continuation sheets used in isolation also double as personal note paper. The type was woodletter from The Typography Workshop's own collection, each item of which is unique, and the stationery was printed letterpress.

Client
Signus Ltd

Design company
HDR Design

Brief
Like many UK companies involved in the high technology industries, digital data specialist Signus is based outside London. When it briefed HDR Design to create a range of stationery, it requested that the design should reflect the fact that its work is technical in nature, but also that the firm is based in the countryside.

Solution
This marriage of technology and nature was achieved by HDR Design through a combination of typography and illustration. Four separate letterheads were created, one for each season of the year, and each to come into service on a certain, pre-arranged date in the year. Each letterhead is a different colour and carries a different illustration of the company's offices in its bottom left-hand corner.

On the green Spring letterhead, the branches on the trees outside carry blossom; on the yellow Summer letterhead, they have a full covering of leaves; by the brown Autumn letterhead, some of these have fallen to the ground, and by the blue winter letterhead, the branches are bare.

Throughout the year, however, the typography, which is rational and ordered remains consistent. Vertical and horizontal lines printed onto the sheet divide columns of information, the rigid structure metaphorically representing the way in which digital data is handled by the company.

Signus Limited

Bradbourne House
East Malling
Kent ME19 6DZ
United Kingdom

Telephone
0732 875 000 general
0732 875 111 direct

Telefax
0732 875 333

John Clements
Type Services Manager

Client
Michelle Turriani

Design company
Angus Hyland

Brief
In the tradition of artists the world over,
Michelle Turriani, an Italian-born photographer
based in London, regularly trades his services
as a photographer for payment in kind: when
he wanted a letterhead, he approached
Pentagram partner Angus Hyland, offering to
swap the design work for a portrait photograph.
Other than the fact that Turriani could not
afford to pay a great deal for paper or printing,
Hyland was given a free reign in his design.


```
HEADED LETTER PAPER
DIN A4 210MM X 297MM
SCHREIBMASCHINENSCHRIFT
PMS RED 032 U
OFFSET LITHOGRAPHY
DESIGNED BY ANGUS HYLAND
PRINTED BY LITHO MAGIC LTD

MICHELLE TURRIANI
13 MORNINGTON AVENUE
LONDON W14 8UJ
UNITED KINGDOM
TELEPHONE NUMBER
+44 (0) 171 6037729
```

Solution

Hyland recognised that it would be a great help to Turriani if he did not have to pay for printing at all. As a result, and in the general spirit of the enterprise, he approached a printer with the offer to include the printer's name on the letterhead in a swap for its services. This in turn led to Hyland including his own name on the letterhead. From here, it was a short conceptual step – and Hyland felt justified in making conceptual steps in view of the fact that Turriani is an artist – to include the DIN specifications of the paper and the name of the typeface used: Schreibmaschinenschrift. Hyland chose the font for two reasons.

First, it was appropriate: a basic, unpretentious typeface was suited to a simple letterhead. Second, the fact that its name was to be printed on the letterhead gave resonance to the fact that it's called 'typewriter writing' – the font explains itself just as the letterhead explains who it was designed by, who printed it and what size it is. The copy was placed in the top left-hand corner merely because that is where the eye naturally turns first when reading. The overall result is a letterhead that is simple in appearance while subtly conveying a range of information not just about its 'owner' but also about itself.

```
BUSINESS CARD
55MM X 85MM
SCHREIBMASCHINENSCHRIFT
PMS RED 032 U
OFFSET LITHOGRAPHY
DESIGNED BY ANGUS HYLAND
PRINTED BY LITHO MAGIC LTD

MICHELLE TURRIANI
13 MORNINGTON AVENUE
LONDON W14 8UJ
UNITED KINGDOM
TELEPHONE NUMBER
+44 (0) 171 6037729
```

```
COMPLIMENTS SLIP
1/3 A4 210MM X 99MM
SCHREIBMASCHINENSCHRIFT
PMS RED 032 U
OFFSET LITHOGRAPHY
DESIGNED BY ANGUS HYLAND
PRINTED BY LITHO MAGIC LTD

MICHELLE TURRIANI
13 MORNINGTON AVENUE
LONDON W14 8UJ
UNITED KINGDOM
TELEPHONE NUMBER
+44 (0) 171 6037729
```

Client
Typography Workshop

Design company
Alan Kitching

Brief
Alan Kitching at the Typography Workshop
frequently redesigns his own stationery, printing
around two hundred copies of each version by
hand, on a letterpress. The letterheads
themselves act as an effective promotional
tool, showing the effects that can be achieved
through the use of letterpress typography, so it
is important to Kitching to demonstrate variety.
One of the advantages of letterpress as a
printing method is that for short print runs it
can be less expensive than using a litho press.
Furthermore, each item printed on a letterpress
is unique, in a way that a computer-designed,
litho-printed sheet can only imitate.

The Typography Workshop
31 Clerkenwell Close London EC1R 0AT
T 0171 490 4586 F 0171 336 7061

Alan Kitching RDI AGI

Solution
In the examples shown here, the name Typography Workshop is abbreviated to parody the way Web addresses are written – the irony being that letterpress, having been in use for hundreds of years, is rather older than the World Wide Web. The name 'Typography Workshop' is written using woodletter blocks, which, being individual and unique, create the slightly rough-hewn effect, while the typographic ornaments scattered around the sheet demonstrate a little of the variety of type that the studio owns.

The business cards, set in Wallbaum and Futura Bold, have a classic, restrained look. The range contains both landscape and portrait format letterheads, compliments slips and business cards,

The Typography Workshop
31 Clerkenwell Close London EC1R 0AT
Telephone 0171 490 4386
Facsimile 0171 336 7061

Alan Kitching RDI AGI

Typ.W/Shop

Alan Kitching RDI AGI
31 Clerkenwell Close London EC1R 0AT
T 0171 490 4386 F 0171 336 7061

Client
Minimum

Design company
Struktur Design

Brief
Minimum, a Danish men's clothing shop, was aware of the clean, modern and functional design philosophy of Struktur Design when it commissioned the company to create an identity and stationery system. Knowing the company's work allowed the client to leave the brief open, safe in the knowledge that its style and design thinking were appropriate.

Solution

Struktur Design chose to create a typographic play on the company's name: although the name itself was printed large, in an apparent conflict of appearance and sense, the design of the type itself echoes the meaning of the word, as its horizontal length is reduced through the use of specially created and unusual ligatures (the connecting links that join two type characters together). The 'i' is made from the vertical stroke of the 'n', for example.

The 'minimum' mark is printed in the top right-hand corner of the sheet, so that it sits on the line of the first fold and can be read as the letter appears from the envelope. In yet another play on the company name, an abbreviation of the word minimum – 'min' – was applied to business cards, some of which were printed on polypropylene, others on card. The typeface used throughout is the sans serif Akzidenz Grotesk.

Client
Tim Rich

Design company
MetaDesign

Brief
Tim Rich is a writer working both as a
journalist and a copywriter for blue-chip
corporate companies. His area of speciality is
design and, as such, he needed a stationery
system that would on the one hand appeal to
designers, expressing his own creative
credentials, but that on the other hand would
also impress corporate clients with his
reliability and professionalism. The effect he
wanted was both classical and creative.

Tim Rich, Writer

Tim Rich, Writer

Third floor
19 Garrick Street
Covent Garden
London WC2E 9AX

Third floor
19 Garrick Street
Covent Garden
London WC2E 9AX

T +44 (0)171 836 6308
F +44 (0)171 836 4811

T +44 (0)171 836 6308
F +44 (0)171 836 4811

Tim Rich, Writer

Tim Rich, Writer

Third floor
19 Garrick Street
Covent Garden
London WC2E 9AX

Third floor
19 Garrick Street
Covent Garden
London WC2E 9AX

T +44 (0)171 836 6308
F +44 (0)171 836 4811

T +44 (0)171 836 6308
F +44 (0)171 836 4811

Tim Rich, Writer

Tim Rich, Writer

Third floor
19 Garrick Street
Covent Garden
London WC2E 9AX

Third floor
19 Garrick Street
Covent Garden
London WC2E 9AX

T +44 (0)171 836 6308
F +44 (0)171 836 4811

T +44 (0)171 836 6308
F +44 (0)171 836 4811

Tim Rich, Writer

Tim Rich, Writer

Third floor
19 Garrick Street
Covent Garden
London WC2E 9AX

Third floor
19 Garrick Street
Covent Garden
London WC2E 9AX

T +44 (0)171 836 6308
F +44 (0)171 836 4811

T +44 (0)171 836 6308
F +44 (0)171 836 4811

Solution
Because Rich's business is words and writing, MetaDesign felt that a purely typographic letterhead would be appropriate. The designers took the initials of the name under which Rich trades – Tim Rich Writer – as the starting point for the identity. The letters 'R' and 'W' were applied to letterheads, while 'T' was applied to continuation sheets. The three letters were all applied at random to both business cards and compliments slips. The letters were printed in black (double hit on the reverse of the sheet to increase show through) on white, as these colours are traditionally associated with writing.

The letterforms are set in Courier, which was also specified as the typeface in which the letters themselves should be written. Although the letters would be written on a computer and laser printed, Courier is a traditional typewriter font, and its use again references the nature of Tim Rich's business while giving a 'classical' impression.

Client
Burrell Architects

Design company
Bell

Brief
Realising that the stationery he was using was
impersonal and anonymous enough to belong
to a firm of accountants or solicitors, architect
James Burrell commissioned Bell to design
a letterhead and business card that reflected
both his professionalism and his creativity.
Burrell was also hoping to make the career
leap from being employed to do detail work on
other designers' buildings, to winning his own
commissions, and hoped that the impression
made by the right stationery design would help
inspire confidence in his abilities.

Solution

Designer Nick Bell's first suggestion was to add the plural 'Architects' to Burrell's trading name. The name was then presented intelligently and attractively in carefully deconstructed Franklin Gothic Bold 2. Bell had selected a translucent paper stock in order that, once it had been printed on both sides, an impression of three-dimensionality would be created, tying in with the nature of Burrell's work.

The show-through effect created by the paper choice also has the effect of creating a highlighted window around the typographic design of Burrell's name, allowing it to dominate the page. On the face of the business card the typographic treatment of Burrell's name is offset to similar effect and impact by the use of a metallic ink.

Client
Johann Kaiser

Design company
HDR Design

Brief
Jewellery making is typically a small-scale
activity involving finely honed craft skills and
infinite precision. Johann Kaiser, a German
jewellery manufacturer, is an exception to the
rule. The company mass-produces wedding
rings and wanted the scale of its operations to
be reflected in the stationery it commissioned
HDR Design to create. As a family business,
Johann Kaiser has a long history in the
manufacture of jewellery, but the latest
generation of the family to take over the
company is keen to show that it is looking to
the future as well as being aware of the past,
another quality it wanted to express through
its stationery.

Solution

Hans Dieter Reichart, a German based in the UK and the founder of HDR Design, based the letterhead on the DIN system devised in 1920s Germany (although there were certain prescribed elements, such as fold marks, which were omitted from the design). The DIN specifications were adhered to because Reichart felt that the neutrality inherent in norms was more fitting for a big company – and conveying the size of the business was a key aspect of the brief.

Furthermore, the openness of the design reflects an openness in the company. It was also felt that using the DIN system allowed the logo, redesigned and refined at the same time as the stationery was created, to stand out, giving it a greater responsibility in expressing the personality of the company. Reichart also believes that clarity – a function of using the DIN specifications – is itself in a sense 'futuristic', as it allows clear communication in an age of information overload.

This particular letterhead had to contend with more information than usual as it was produced in two languages, English and German, reflecting the fact the Johann Kaiser has an American daughter company. All of the text on the stationery system was set in Univers, a typeface selected for its international, classic modern qualities.

JohannKaiser

Herstellung von Trauringen und
Diamantschmuck aus Gold und Platin
*Manufacturer of rings and jewelry
made of gold and platinum*

JohannKaiser
Herstellung von Trauringen und
Diamantschmuck aus Gold und Platin

Anne Kaiser-Kolb
Geschäftsführer
Managing Director

Hauptstraße 149
D-63512 Hainburg
Germany
T: +49 (0)61 82 95 09 0
F: +49 (0)51 82 95 09 23
http://www.jk-kaiser.com

JohannKaiser GmbH   Postfach *POB* 1080   D-63506 Hainburg   *Germany*

Hauptstraße 149
D-63512 Hainburg
Germany
T: +49 (0)61 82 95 09 0
F: +49 (0)61 82 95 09 23
http://www.jk-kaiser.com

Ihr Zeichen
Your reference

Unser Zeichen
Our reference

Betrifft
Regarding

Datum
Date

Aufträge (24 Std):
Orders (24 h):
T: +49 (0)61 82 95 09 90

Service:
T: +49 (0)61 82 95 09 81

Buchhaltung:
Accounting:
T: +49 (0)61 82 95 09 82

Sparkasse Langen-Seligenstadt:
BLZ: 506 521 24
Ktn-Nr.: 16 004 814
Volksbank Hausen
BLZ: 505 613 15
Kto-Nr.: 3603 011

Dresdner Bank Seligenstadt
BLZ: 506 800 05
Ktn-Nr.: 580 187 400
Postbank Frankfurt
BLZ: 500 100 60
Kto-Nr.: 94 01-601

Johann Kaiser Trauring
und Schmuck GmbH
Sitz und Gerichtsstand Hainburg
Amtsgericht Seligenstadt HRB 1019
Beidseitiger Erfüllungsort ist
Hainburg, USt-IdNr.: DE811215208

Geschäftsführung:
Managing Directors:
Anna Margarete Kaiser-Kolb
Dipl.-Volkswirt Wolfgang Kolb

104–129
Surface Effects

Clements Ribeiro Limited 48 South Molto

Client
Clements Ribeiro

Design company
Area

Brief
A common response to a naïve style in art and
design is 'a child could have done that'. In the
case of London-based fashion design duo
Clements Ribeiro, the critics would have been
right. The company's logo, which the designers
had originally wanted to look slightly rough
and ready, was designed by a child of their
acquaintance.

After it had been in use for a while, however, the pair realised that the mark was not entirely appropriate or relevant to the direction their work was taking, and that while they wanted to maintain the essential air of naïvety in the type and illustration, they wanted it to be more controlled and slick-looking.

Solution
Area based its new logo on the original – tweaking elements to give it more uniformity and control. The letter heights, which had previously varied wildly, were brought more into line, and the 'drip' effect was re-drawn. The logo as a whole was then applied to the letterhead and the unusually shaped business card using four-colour litho printing.

The whole design, including the finest threads of line in the illustration, was then embossed, making the sheet interesting to both the eye and the touch.

CLEMENTS
RIBEIRO

Clements Ribeiro Limited
48 South Molton Street London w1y 1he
Tel 0171 409 7719 Fax 0171 409 1741

Client
Digital Print

Design company
Wild & Frey

Brief
Zürich-based specialist printer Digital Print is
a master of its craft, and offers such services
as die-cutting, embossing and varnishing to
a high degree of precision and quality of finish.
When it commissioned Wild & Frey to create
its stationery, it wanted the design not only
to emphasise its quality and status within the
printing industry, but also to show off some
of its skills.

Solution
The project started with the creation of a company logo. Rather than create a rigid, inflexible mark, the designers adopted a shape - a rectangle - that could be applied to all of the communications and be used to demonstrate the various techniques practiced by Digital Print. Wild & Frey applied the mark to a letterhead, business cards, envelopes in a range of sizes, and a 'good for printing sheet' (which is attached to a proof whose quality is sufficient that it is passed for print).

Each item was given a different printing treatment, so that the range as a whole covers silk-screen printing, die-cutting, embossing, varnishes, reverse printing (where the mark is applied to the back of the sheet) and hot-foil stamping (the application of a metallic strip). A match book was also created for promotional purposes, on which the striking surface was in the rectangular shape.

This demonstrated a rare level of dedication on the part of both designer and client as a company capable of making the match book to those specifications could be found no closer to home than Japan. The stationery range as a whole is a good example of how unity can be given to an identity system by something no more sophisticated than a simple shape, which in turn allows the designers the freedom to create something beautiful, functional and memorable.

Client
The Savoy

Design company
Pentagram

Brief
The Savoy is one of London's grandest hotels, with an international clientele and a special place in the heart of anyone who has ever eaten in its Grill Room. Design company Pentagram, which has worked extensively with the hotel's owners, Savoy Hotels, was invited to pitch for a redesign of the hotel's identity, including its stationery system.

Solution

Taking as its cue the hotel's proximity to 'theatreland' in London's West End, and its tradition of feeding and accommodating the grandees of the stage, Pentagram chose 'theatricality' as a keyword, reflecting both the larger-than-life people who stay there and the look of the hotel, which itself was revamped in the 1930s and is a classic example of art deco design. The hotel's striped awning is a London landmark, and designer John Rushworth was amazed to find that its familiar sans serif lettering, with an enlarged 'V', had never been used on stationery before. He turned the lettering into the hotel's logotype, and applied it to the letterhead through die stamping.

The mottled, varied tones of the ink applied through die-stamping, and the expense of the process itself, gave the requisite feel of quality that would not have been achieved through simply embossing a litho-printed sheet. The die-stamping process, as well as the asymmetric typography, subtly refer to the 1930s, the decade in which the hotel itself was styled. The business card shown here is in both English and Japanese, and several other bi-lingual variations were produced to cater for the hotel's international clientele.

SAVOY LONDON

General Manager's Office
The Savoy
Strand
London WC2R 0EU
Tel 0171 856 4545
Fax 0171 240 6040

SAVOY LONDON

Duncan R. Palmer
General Manager
ジェネラル マネージャー
ダンカン・パーマー

The Savoy
Strand, London
WC2R 0EU
ザ・サヴォイ

The Savoy Hotel Plc.
Registered in England
No. 29022
Registered Office
1 Savoy Hill
London WC2R 0BP

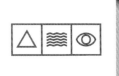

3mv Limited. Unit 4E/F West Point
33-34 Warple Way, London W3 ORX
Telephone: 081 740.5959
Fax: 081 740.5943

Phil Clift
Operations Director

Registered Office: as above
Registered no: 2458646

Solution
Area designer Richard Smith began to
research numerology and found that the name
3mv could be represented pictorially through
the numerological meanings of the numbers
and letters in Greek and Hebrew. Thus, from
the Greek the '3' became a triangle, and from
the Hebrew the 'M' becomes water and the
'V' an eye.

As these were printed on the sheet in a bright
orange, the name 3mv, which was blind
embossed onto the opposite side of the page
is only seen secondarily, adding an element
of surprise and mystery to the proceedings.

3mv Limited. Unit 4E/F West Point
33-34 Warple Way, London W3 0RX
Telephone: 081 740 5959
Fax: 081 740 5943

Brief
Struktur Design was commissioned to design
an identity and stationery range for a Danish
women's wear company, dias, whose name is
Greek for 'through'. The stationery had to look
feminine, as its business is women's wear, but
its owners also wanted a look that was clean
and modern – in other words, no flowers or
other supposedly 'feminine' imagery.

dias den

Solution
The designers used the Greek meaning of the word dias as a concept, printing the name on the reverse of the sheet so that it shows through. The use of 60 gsm Bible paper as the stock facilitated this, while the use of 'subtle' colours in the reverse printing is in reference to the business of dias.

Metallic inks were used on both the letterhead and the business cards (which were made of tracing paper). Some of the business cards were printed in solid colour, with the name dias reversed out, while others had the name printed onto them, allowing light to shine through.

Client
Blast

Design company
Blast

Brief
When design company Blast came to design its own stationery, the designers wanted the letterhead and business card to convey the personality of the company, which is professional but fun. Like the personality of the company itself, the stationery should work on two levels: on one level the image should be one of attractive professionalism, but on another, there should be something to engage the interest of the readers, and encourage them to interact with the stationery, and by extension the design company, on a more light-hearted and entertaining level.

bla s t

55 farringdon road
clerkenwell london ec1m 3jb

tel + 0171 242 9565

up and atom!

bla s t

55 farringdon road clerkenwell london ec1m 3jb

tel + 0171 242 9565   fax + 0171 242 4668   isdn + 0171 831 6318

Solution
By printing on the reverse side of the sheet, Blast turned what is usually a design problem – show-through – into a feature. While the front of the sheet fulfils the first part of the requirements of the brief – that the letterhead should look professional – when the sheet is lifted to the light the reader is able to see an image which connects with the name of the company. Although the designers opted for conventional litho printing, the use of two special colours – a silver and an orange 'as bright as the printer could mix it' – rather than the usual four-colour process added to the sense of fun and sparkle that the designers wished to create.

As with the letterheads, the designers wanted the business cards to appear at once professional but also fun, with the added benefit that recipients would be more likely to keep them. These were also printed in orange and silver, and as a finishing touch, the name Blast was echoed by the addition of a length of caps of the sort normally used in toy guns, which encourage the recipient to interact with the card by setting fire to it. While the use of special colours and printing on both faces of the letterhead and business cards did add to the drying time, the job did not prove to be significantly more expensive than a conventional letterhead.

fold back stand
place on flat surface

stand well back

light tip of fuse

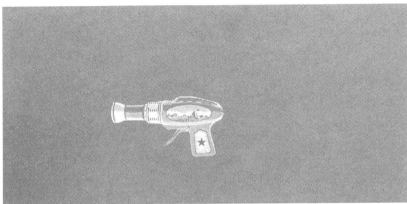

Client
Radioactive Ink

Design company
Werner Design Works

Brief
As relative newcomers to the business, the
two writers for radio who comprise Radioactive
Ink needed an identity to set them apart from
the competition. As most of their business
comes from advertising agencies, the letterhead
needed to be fresh and fun but, as the duo were
not yet firmly financially established, it had to
be inexpensive.

RADIOACTIVE INK
105 EAST ELMWOOD PLACE
MINNEAPOLIS, MN 55419
FACSIMILE (612) 823
PHONE (612)

Solution
The punning name Radioactive was conceived by the writers themselves, but it gave the designers at Werner Design Works their cue for the letterhead. It was decided to present the writers as a slightly risky alternative to the norm, in a reverse psychology move calculated to get advertising agencies itching to hire them. This presentation was achieved through packaging the letterhead itself as a radioactive document. A silver-backed paper stock suggesting radiation-proof material was sourced, and a blue dot printed on the reverse of the sheet by letterpress.

The effect was completed with adhesive stickers bearing a radioactivity warning on an orange background which were printed at a high-street copy shop extremely cheaply. These can then be attached not only to the letterhead but to any other communications the duo send out.

RADIOACTIVE INK
105 EAST ELMWOOD PLACE
MINNEAPOLIS, MN 55419
FACSIMILE (612) 822-3854

MARK BENNINGHOFEN

Phone (612) 822-3854

Brief
It is a commonly heard complaint that high-street retailers don't cater for the larger woman. Filling that niche in the market is Anna Scholtz, a fashion designer who makes sexy clothes for big women. When she commissioned Alan Dye of Alan Dye Associates to design her stationery, the one requirement was that the identity, like her clients, should be big and bold.

120 121

Solution
Dye took his client at her word, running the name Anna Scholtz, set in Franklin Gothic, across the top of the sheet. Bringing an element of the sexiness of the clothes into the design, Dye decided to print the surname using a silver foil block.

Based on his past experience with foil blocking, which, like many surface treatments, can cause lighter papers to crumple and buckle, Dye requested that the printer, Gavin Martin Associates, use a stock that was sufficiently heavy to take the foil block without crumpling.

Unit 9. 81 Southern Row
London W10 5AL
Great Britain
T+44(0)181 964 3040
F+44(0)181 964 5020

Client
Opal Sky

Design company
Viva Dolan

Brief
Based in Toronto, Canada, Opal Sky is a
software design firm whose main product
controls bookings and analyses databases for
the travel industry. Viva Dolan had worked for
the company in a previous incarnation and the
strength of the designer/client relationship
allowed Opal Sky to leave the brief open,
although as a new start-up business, it was
agreed that its letterhead should reflect that
although the company is young and at the
cutting edge of the industry, it also has an
understanding of the history of the technology.

O P A L   S K Y

Solution
The sense of historical perspective was introduced through the flexible mark designed for Opal Sky by Viva Dolan. The spirograph, which is printed on the reverse of the sheet, has associations with the 1960s, although it is not specifically rooted in any one time. This glance back in time was counterbalanced through a combination of paper choice and printing techniques to give the stationery a contemporary feel. A translucent stock was selected, allowing the mark on the reverse of the sheet to show through.

The mark itself is reversed out of solid colour, and a special silver ink was chosen to give the letterhead an appropriately hi-tech feel. The business cards were also printed in silver on Gilclear paper, a heavy card stock that is semi-translucent. Only two colours are used on the face of the sheet, creating an overall impression of clean modernity with a twist.

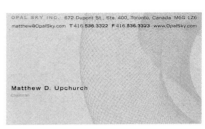

Client
Cloud Nine

Design company
The Partners

Brief
Introduction agencies often have slightly cheap and tacky associations in the mind of the general public, and it was these that the founder of a new agency wished to dispel when she briefed design company The Partners to create a name and visual manifestation for her business. The image she wished to project was of a high-class agency that was serious about its work but at the same time human and sympathetic. As the agency's clients would be of both sexes, the name and identity should appeal equally to both men and women.

Solution
The name Cloud Nine was suggested by The Partners as it was felt to be suitably restrained yet hinted at the aspirational nature of the agency's potential clients – the name refers to the term for happiness, being on cloud nine, and also has connotations of stature and quality. When it came to creating the stationery itself, the designers wanted to avoid the clichéd route of hearts and flowers, which would have been inappropriate for the image the agency wished to project. Instead, a logo was created by placing figure 9s end on end to create a cloud shape.

The logo was applied to the letterhead through embossing, a technique which, it was felt, had associations of quality and up-scale positioning and also of care and precision – necessary qualities when dealing in affairs of the heart.

Client
Helengai Harbottle

Design company
johnson banks

Brief
Helengai Harbottle is a textile designer specialising in knitwear. She approached johnson banks to create a logo and stationery range for her business. The logo, based on a set of interlocking 'H's, came from the initials of her name and is reminiscent of the knitting process in appearance. Both Harbottle and the designers felt that the logo should be large and prominent on the letterhead, but the challenge came in finding a way to do this without interfering with its functionality.

Helengai Harbottle 2nd Floor 110-112 Curtain Road London EC2 3AH Tel/Fax 0171 729 9546

Solution
In order to show the logo large, without limiting the amount of space left for typing, the designers opted to print it on the reverse of the sheet, creating a show-through effect. The decision to reverse the letters out of black, rather than just printing them onto the back of the sheet, meant that extra care had to be taken with the choice of printer – johnson banks took the job to a firm specialised in high-end, quality work – and also that the paper had to be sealed before printing began, in order that it did not soak up too much of the back ink. The fact that the printing and drying processes would take longer than usual was also taken into account.

Helengai Harbottle 2nd Floor 110-112 Curtain Road London EC2 3AH Tel/Fax 0171 729 9546

Client
Art Directors' Collective

Design company
Area

Brief
ADC stands for the Art Directors' Collective,
a floating pool of creatives who can be hired
to work on a variety of media projects in areas
such as television programming, advertising
and photography. The group is run by
sponsorship and marketing expert Anthony
Fawcett and ex-Eurythmics guitarist and
photographer Dave Stewart. As the exact nature
of what the group does is imprecise – they will
consider a wide variety of projects – it was
important that the stationery should not define
them too closely. The Art Directors' Collective
also wanted it to have a cool, modern, yet
professional image.

2c
D'Art
London
W1V 3FH
Telephone
071 734 0020
Facsimile
071 287 3089

David A Stewart
Anthony Fawcett

Solution
Area created a logo of solid, graphic shapes based on the group's initials, which was applied to the top corner of the sheet. The brief's demand for subtlety and sophistication was met by applying the mark using a spot varnish in a colour only marginally different from that of the paper stock.

Despite the similarity in colour, the logo is easily distinguished because its gloss finish stands out from a matt background. The two similar colours soften the heavy, bold letter shapes, enhancing the image of sleek sophistication the Art Directors' Collective wanted to project.

Menno Witt Schoonmaakbedrijf   Wij

Tel

Uden A
Televisior
Unit 3
Chelsea W
Lots Road
London SW

T +44 171
F +44 171

ok tapijtreiniging wassen van ramen reiniging van gevels brand en roetreini

25 80 Autotel 06 5333 3286 V

Menno Witt Afdc

Client
Canna Kendall & Co

Design company
johnson banks

Brief
Canna Kendall is a firm of advertising
headhunters based in London. Although the
firm itself is just starting out in the advertising
recruitment game, and needed its stationery to
arrest the attention of its recipients, its founders
have been in the industry for a long time and
knew how their potential clients thought. When
the company commissioned design company
johnson banks to create a range of stationery
materials, the brief was simple, if demanding:
the company asked only that whatever
stationery johnson banks designed, it should
be good enough to win a prestigious D&AD
(design and advertising) Award.

CANNA KENDALL & CO. 83 Charlotte Street London W1P 1LB

Telephone 0171 580 3455 Facsimile 0171 580 2974

BEVERLEY PARKER

Solution
As Canna Kendall's business is in matching suitable employees with suitable employers, johnson banks took the theme of complementary partners for the stationery. Across a range of business cards, as well as both A4 and A5 letterheads, the designers created four sets of matched pairs: fish and chips, popeye and olive, dog and bone and egg and bacon. A further element of humour was injected into the images in that some of the supposedly matched pairs only appear to be so: popeye's olive is not his cartoon girlfriend but a small green fruit.

The photographs were taken by advertising photographer Mike Parsons. The images proved to be a success, with clients asking for full sets of the business cards at meetings. The flexible format has also lent itself to other materials such as a Christmas card on which pine needles were twinned with a vacuum cleaner. The stationery did indeed go on to win a Silver Award at D&AD, giving Canna Kendall some much-appreciated publicity in its target market.

CANNA KENDALL & CO. 83 Charlotte Street London W1P 1LB

Telephone 0171 580 3455 Facsimile 0171 580 2974

Client
Glassworks

Design company
Frost Design

Brief
Glassworks is a film-production house, based
at the heart of the UK's TV and commercials
industry in Soho, London. The company is
confident in its size, reputation and creativity
and as a consequence, when it commissioned
Frost Design to create an identity and stationery
system, the brief was left relatively open: all
that was required was that the stationery was
appropriate, given the sector in which the
company does business – its main clients are
the local advertising agencies – and that it
should look good.

Solution
Taking the company's name as the basis for its solution, Frost Design commissioned a model maker to build a letter 'G' in blocks of glass. This was then photographed by Matthew Donaldson, a regular collaborator with the design consultancy, and the image, which has slightly abstract qualities, was applied directly to the reverse of the letterhead.

The soft, green tones of the photograph have a modern, minimal look which would strike a chord with the aesthetically and visually aware denizens of ad-land. The 'G' logo was later applied more widely, including frosting it onto glass doors at the company's offices and creating a pair of table legs in a 'G' shape for its reception desk.

Client
Q101

Design company
Segura Inc.

Brief
An alternative music station needs an
alternative stationery system and when
Chicago-based Q101 Radio commissioned
Segura Inc. to create its letterhead, compliments
slip and business card, it asked for something
that was slightly edgy and different.

Solution
Segura Inc. realised that although the image
of the radio station suggested a very radical
design, the recipients of the letterhead would
mostly be potential clients such as buyers
of advertising space, and aimed to create a
letterhead that was radical and contemporary
without being off-putting to corporate clients.
The solution was found in illustration.
Screen grabs were taken from music videos,
distressed to the point where they are almost
unrecognisable, and layered to create a visual
impression of the sort of music played on the
station that is at once attractive to listeners,
and acceptable to its clients.

The illustration forms a border to the sheet,
framing the area in which the letter is written
and emphasising it through the contrast
between the dark illustration and the white
paper stock. The words 'Alternative New Music'
are embedded within the border, adding a
typographic element to the illustration. Similar
illustrations were applied to continuation sheets,
compliments slips, folding cards, envelopes,
lined note paper and adhesive labels.

EMMIS Broadcasting Corp. WKQX-FM Merchandise Mart Plaza Ste. 1700 Chicago, IL 60654 Tel: 312.527.8348 Fax: 312.527.5682

Client
Hannah S. Fricke

Design company
Factor Design

Brief
As an advertising copywriter, Hannah Fricke
deals with advertising agencies as an everyday
part of her business. It is to those agencies
that most of her written communications are
sent and it was an important aspect of the
design of her stationery that it should
demonstrate her knowledge of the industry
and of her own craft – writing.

Solution

On the front of the sheet, a numbered scale like the ones found, for example, in word processing packages, runs along the top and down the side of the page, which is intended to imply that Fricke can write copy to fit – an important skill for a copywriter. In order to further demonstrate Fricke's awareness of the needs of an advertising agency, Factor Design commissioned illustrator Tanja Jacobs to create a funny, cartoon-like illustration showing the communication networks that exist within an advertising agency.

This was then printed on the reverse of the sheet. The illustration and the choice of a rich, dark stock also combine to give the stationery a warm, attractive 'personality'.

Client
Harbourside

Design company
Bell

Brief
As part of a plan to develop the disused docks
of the city of Bristol in South West England, the
Arts Council, a government-funded body,
announced a plan to build an arts centre. The
building itself was to be designed by Behnisch
and Behnisch, an internationally renowned
architectural practice, and the task of designing
an identity and stationery for the scheme fell to
graphic design consultancy Bell. In order to
secure funding for the proposed project, it was
important to convince the fund-holding bodies,
such as the Arts Council and the National
Lottery, that the scheme would be as much a
resource for the people of South West England
as for the artists themselves.

the **harbourside** centre

the harbourside centre 2 st. george's court st. george's road bristol bs1 5ug united kingdom
phone +44 (0)117 925 5252 fax +44 (0)117 925 5250
director duncan fraser chairman louis sherwood

Registered Charity no: 1054023 Vat no: 682279013 Registered Company no: 3133490
Registered Office: The Harbourside Centre Limited Narrow Quay House Prince Street Bristol BS1 4AH

SUPPORTED BY
THE NATIONAL LOTTERY
THROUGH
THE ARTS COUNCIL
OF ENGLAND

Solution
With the idea in mind that the identity should suggest a blurring of boundaries between artist and spectator, designer Nick Bell decided against creating a logo of the 'graphic stamp' variety in favour of a mark that represented a coming together of parts. The tonal scale of blues that eventually became the mark is based on an architectural feature of the centre itself, despite the fact that it did not exist when the stationery was designed. One wall of the proposed building was to be made of glass, and overlooked the harbour from which it takes its name.

This would allow light reflected from the water to create patterns on the ceiling inside the building. From the image of a shifting body of water, Bell created the block of blues that acts as the centre's mark. A further reference to the building itself was made through positioning the mark underneath the word 'harbourside'. The ascenders of the letters 'h', 'b' and 'd' and the dot of the letter 'i' are 'mirrored in the mark below, suggesting the reflection of an architectural skyline and the sun in the water of the harbour. Unfortunately, despite the best efforts of both architect and graphic designer, the Arts Council pulled out of the project before completion, pleading poverty.

Sue Sanctuary Marketing Assistant

the harbourside centre
2 st. george's court st. george's road
bristol bs1 5ug united kingdom

phone +44 (0)117 925 5252 fax +44 (0)117 925 5250

with compliments from the harbourside centre 2 st. george's court st. george's road bristol bs1 5ug united kingdom
phone +44 (0)117 925 5252 fax +44 (0)117 925 5250

Client
Tilney Shane

Design company
Pyott Design

Brief
Companies involved in the creative industries
often have a problem finding a way to
express that they are both creative and
also professional and organised.

142 143

When Tilney Shane, a firm of architectural and interior designers, commissioned Pyott Design to create a range of stationery, it stressed the importance of communicating that it was both highly creative and imaginative, but also practical in terms of project management and co-ordination.

Solution
A sense of professionalism and pragmatism was lent to the stationery through the use of a rigid grid structure and tidy typography. It was in the illustration, however, that Tilney Shane's creativity was expressed. The twelve images, which were applied to letterheads, compliments slips and business cards, were created from scratch using Adobe's Photoshop software. Although abstract, the images are intended to represent some of the raw materials of the building trade: concrete, glass, wood and cloth.

The twelve basic images were given further colour variations in an effort to increase variety to the point where no one image in itself could be said to represent the company, only a type of image. The system is flexible enough to allow almost infinite numbers of further images to be created and added in accordance with changing trends within architecture and interior design in the future.

Client
Uden Associates

Design company
Intro

Brief
Uden Associates, a leading independent
television programme production company,
had a stationery system designed in the 1980s
by 8vo which won many plaudits from within
and without the design industry. However, as
TV programming in the UK has changed, with
increasing numbers of programmes made by
small, independent production companies with
a makeshift, do-it-yourself aesthetic, Uden
Associates realised that it was in danger of
being seen as monolithic and wanted to
demonstrate through its stationery that it could
make those kind of programmes as well as the
more serious, high-budget output for which it
was best known.

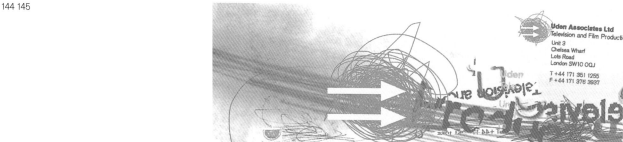

Solution
While the company was not 'dumbing down' in its programme making, it did want to attract new clients and convince existing ones that it was adaptable and aware of the changing market, and it was with this in mind that Intro set out to create a letterhead that emphasised some of the qualities in those new television programmes – spontaneity, speed, and a rough-hewn aesthetic. A range of six distinct business cards suggested spontaneity and non-conformity, while the letterhead itself, printed two-colour instead of the previous four, made use of illustration to create the appropriate effect. Natural objects were scanned into a desktop scanner and manipulated using an Apple Macintosh.

In order to show clients that Uden Associates had not abandoned the serious programme making on which its reputation is founded, this seemingly random, scratchy, computer-manipulated illustration was counterbalanced by clean, Swiss-influenced typography to retain the corporate, professional air.

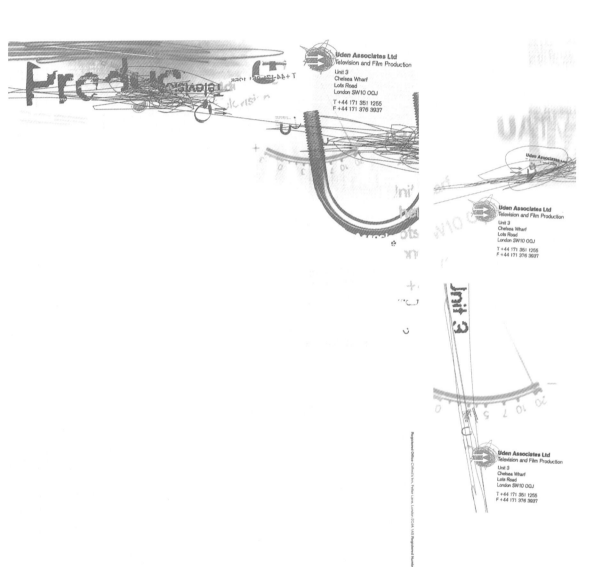

Client
Bluewater

Design company
Glazer Design

Brief
Bluewater is Europe's largest retail
development, and is the first of a new breed
of shopping centres that, as a key part of their
offer, will provide leisure activities such as
bars, cinemas and sporting facilities, turning
the shopping trip into a complete day out for
the whole family. Bluewater's developers,
Lend Lease, needed to convey this distinction
to potential buyers of retail space at the site.
At the time the space was put on the market,
however, the building site itself was little more
than an uninspiring mess of puddles, rubble
and cement trucks.

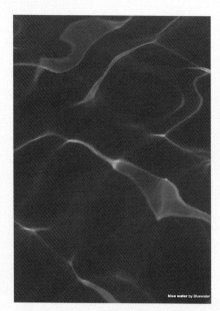

blue water by Bluewater

red roses by Bluewater

Lend Lease, perhaps mindful of the old saying 'never show a fool a half-built house', realised that if the site itself would not inspire potential buyers, it would need to find another way of communicating its vision, and therefore approached design consultancy Glazer to create a range of materials, including a stationery system, through which it could tell customers about the development.

Solution
It can be difficult for someone looking at a project halfway to completion to appreciate that it will look a lot better when it is finished. Glazer Design realised that images of the site as it was would not sell the Bluewater concept to potential customers, and instead sought a different route. The designers took the name Bluewater as the basis of a virtual sensory experience of the site. Other colour-related, emotionally charged concepts were also created: red roses, green grass, brown coffee beans. Each suggested an aspect of a day out at Bluewater.

These images were then applied to letterheads, postcards and business cards, as well as a brochure and trade-press advertising, ensuring that through all communications with potential customers, a solid brand based on a vision was built. The images proved crucial in conveying to potential customers a sense of what the site they were being asked to buy into might be like at completion.

brown beans by Bluewater

Client
Menno Witt

Design company
Interbrand Newell & Sorrell

Brief
Menno Witt cleans the offices of design
company Interbrand Newell & Sorrell's
Amsterdam branch. Office cleaning, however,
is only one part of Witt's business, which also
includes decorating and construction.

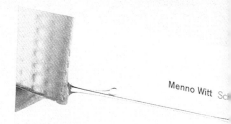

Van Musschenbroekstraat 33 3514 XH Utrecht
Rabobank nr. 34.13.05.286 K.v.K. nr. 3012 4135

Van Musschenbroekstraat 33 3514 XH Utrecht
Rabobank nr. 34.13.05.286 K.v.K. nr. 3012 4135

When, in a table-turning exercise, he sought the services of his client Interbrand Newell & Sorrell to create a new identity and stationery range for him, it was critical that the design should reflect all of his areas of endeavour. Although the two businesses are similar, and Witt wanted to promote both at the same time, he was keen that they should remain distinct.

Solution
The solution was a double-sided stationery range using illustration to distinguish between the businesses. On both the letterhead and the business card, a photograph of a paintbrush dripping vivid blue paint represents the building and decorating arm of the Witt empire, and this is contrasted on the other side of the sheet by a leaking sponge to illustrate the office-cleaning business.

Menno Witt is then able to use whichever side of the letterhead caters for the subject of the letter in question – construction or cleaning – while still making the recipient aware that he is available for other types of work.

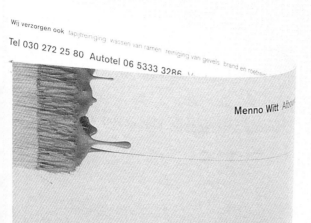

Client
Factor Design

Design company
Factor Design

Brief
Hamburg-based graphic design consultancy
Factor Design saw its own stationery fitting into
a wider scheme of materials produced by the
company, rather like the range of forms in a
bank. To that end, the number 'one' is printed
in the top left-hand corner of the letterhead,
signifying that it is the first in a series of such
forms. This formal concept dictated a formal
design, but the studio also wanted the
letterhead to demonstrate its creativity.

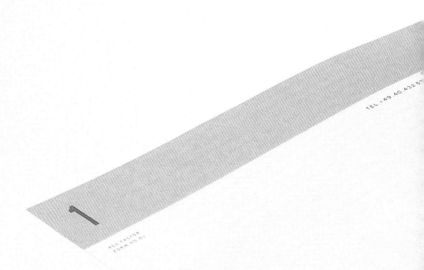

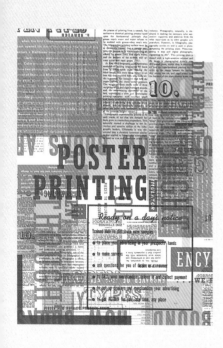

Solution

The solution was found in the use of imagery. The reverse side of the sheet was covered with an illustration reminiscent of the test sheets used by printers to check such things as the spread of ink on the presses. The same sheet is run several times through the press, resulting in a random overlaying of text and images. The process itself was interesting to the designers as it has echoes in some of the design work of the Bauhaus period as well as an aesthetic that developed out of the possibilities introduced by the Macintosh computer.

More significantly, however, the illustration was intended to demonstrate the studio's affinity with the printing process itself, as well as with typography in general. The letterforms used in the illustration were sourced from American printers' catalogues of the 1950s and 60s and, although it is intended to appear random and accidentally beautiful, was actually put together very deliberately.

Client
Printed Stationery

Design company
HGV

Brief
Printed Stationery is a firm of printers whose
main target market is the graphic design
industry. The company wanted a letterhead
that would appeal to designers on their own
terms, showing that Printed Stationery thought
the same way and spoke the same language.
It was also important that the letterhead should
show off the company's capabilities as a printer.

Printed Stationery

326 City Road
London EC1V 2PT
Tel 0171 278 7706
Fax 0171 278 7203

Printed Stationery Limited.
Registered office as above.
Registered No: 2598525

Solution
HGV used blocks of printers' type, photographed by John Edwards, as illustrations to identify the component parts of the stationery system. By using quotation marks to show the start of text, an ampersand to indicate the continuation sheet and so on, the letterhead demonstrates not only that Printed Stationery understands the sort of graphic wit that appeals to designers, but also makes direct reference to the tools of its trade.

The designers experimented with both tri-tone (containing a special silver ink) and duo-tone reproductions of the images, settling eventually for the duo-tone which, it was felt, brought out the qualities of the metal type more effectively.

Ian Swindale

Printed Stationery

326 City Road
London EC1V 2PT
Tel 0171 278 7706
Fax 0171 278 7203

Ade Borishade

Printed Stationery

326 City Road
London EC1V 2PT
Tel 0171 278 7706
Fax 0171 278 7203

with compliments

Printed Stationery

326 City Road
London EC1V 2PT
Tel 0171 278 7706
Fax 0171 278 7203

Client
Quasi

Design company
Birgit Eggers

Brief
Quasi is a group of three photographers
based in the Netherlands. When the group
commissioned graphic designer Birgit Eggers to
create a range of stationery, the photographers
explained that while the items must identify
them as collectively belonging to the group,
their individual creative personalities were
important and should not be entirely subsumed
by one over-arching identity. As well as
letterheads, Eggers was also commissioned to
design a means by which individual members
of the group could send out examples of their
work to potential clients.

Solution
Eggers solved the problem of representing three in one by creating one basic letterhead template, from which three separate varieties were made. Each letterhead carries the name Quasi, and also the name of the group member to whom it belongs. Printed upside-down at the foot of the reverse of the sheet are eleven photographs by all three members of the group. Individuality is achieved through the use of a simple die-cut which, when the sheet is folded, highlights one photograph by the group member, which then appears through the hole right way up next to the name of the member to whom the letterhead belongs.

A5 cards bearing examples of each individual photographer's work were also created.
A scored rectangle in the centre of the card means that the business card can be detached, leaving a cropped photograph on the face of the business card. As in the case of the 'crops' created by the die-cut on the letterhead, this is intended to subliminally reinforce the idea of photography in the mind of the recipient.

Terms & Techniques

Like any semi-industrial activity, stationery design and printing has its fair share of arcane terminology. There follows a concise glossary explaining some terms relating to aspects of stationery design.

Paper comes in many more forms than it is possible to list here, so no attempt has been made to do so. Each paper type has its own qualities and characteristics and will respond differently to different print processes. It is advisable to seek a printer's advice when selecting a paper stock.

A series
Refers to the system of DIN or ISO series of paper sizes.

Bible paper
A very thin paper.

Blind embossing
Embossing without using ink to create a raised area in the paper, visible by the shadow cast by the area in relief.

Coated paper
Paper coated in china clay or similar materials to give it a smooth surface.

Continuation sheet
A secondary sheet to the letterhead, usually identified through elements of the design on the letterhead itself, minus the address and other extraneous detail.

Corporate identity
The process whereby unity is given to the visual manifestations of a company's personality through design, identifying its products, property or communications. At its most basic level, this involves the application of the company's logo or trademark.

Custom making
Also known as 'bespoke'; paper made to a customer's own specifications.

Debossing
A depressed design on the paper created by pressing the sheet between two interlocking blocks, one of which has a raised design on it, the other a matching depression.

Die
An engraved metal stamp used by the printer to cut or otherwise alter the flat surface of the paper.

Die-cut
Area cut from a sheet of paper using a die.

Die stamping
Stamping with a die that leaves an 'embossed' design on the surface of the sheet.

DIN
Abbreviation of Deutsche Industrie Norm, a set of industry standards established in Germany in the 1920s and now used across Europe. Subsequently adopted by the International Standards Organization (ISO).

Double hit
Printing a sheet twice to increase the density of the ink.

Embossing
A raised design on the paper created by pressing the sheet between two interlocking blocks, one of which has a raised design on it, the other a matching depression. See also die stamping, thermography and debossing.

Foil blocking
A process in which a thin layer of metal foil is applied to the surface of a sheet of paper using heat.

Font
Traditional term for a complete set of alphabets relating to one size of typeface, including upper and lower case roman, italics, bolds, figures and punctuation marks.

Four-colour printing
The process of producing printed colour using four separate plates to print yellow, magenta, cyan and black to give an impression of full colour. 'Special' colours such as silvers can be added on successive plates.

gsm
see weight.

House style
A set of guidelines ensuring consistency throughout all of a company's communications.

Ink-jet printer
Computer-linked printing device in which the image is created by high-speed jets of ink.

ISO sizes
see DIN.

Justified
Typographic arrangement in which the letters and words of each line are spaced to fill a particular column width. See ranged left/right.

Laser printer
A common computer-linked desk-top printer in which beams of laser light activate a photoconductive powder, creating an electrostatic image which is transferred to the paper through heat.

Letterhead
The printed design on letter stationery.

Letterpress
A traditional form of relief printing in which ink is applied to the paper through pressure. Raised blocks of type and image are pressed onto the sheet, leaving an impression where they come into contact. Usually used for shorter print runs or very high end jobs.

Litho printing
   The most common letterhead printing process based on the principle that oil and water do not mix. The design, which is treated to be water-resistant but attractive to oil and grease, is transferred to the page from flat plate by means of a rolling cylinder. Also known as offset litho, lithography and photolithography.

Logotype
   Letters or words in a distinctive form, often used as, or as part of a company's logo.

Ranged left/right
   Typographic arrangement in which lines of unequal length are aligned along the left- or right-hand margin, with a ragged effect on the opposite margin.

Reverse printing
   Printing on the reverse face of the letterhead sheet, often with the intention of creating a show-through effect.

Roman typeface
   Typeface whose main strokes are capped by a terminal stroke.

Sans serif typeface
   Typeface whose letters lack a terminal stroke at the top and bottom of the main strokes of a Roman typeface.

Screen printing
   A process evolved from the traditional silk-screen method. The ink is applied to the sheet through a fine screen made of fabric or metal. The process has the advantage of being able to print on materials other than paper such as plastic and metal.

Thermography
   A raised, glossy surface is created by sprinkling resin onto wet ink.

Trademark
   A logotype or symbol used to identify the products, property or communications of a particular company.

Tooth
   The rough texture of the paper surface.

Typeface
   Alphabet created for the purposes of printing.

Typography
   The arrangement and specification of type for printing.

Vellum
   Paper made from calf skin, or fine parchment papers which imitate this.

Watermark
   Design within the paper itself, created by pressing a pattern into the sheet while it is still wet, thinning it in that area and allowing light to shine through.

Weight
   The weight of a paper, which is influenced by its thickness and density, is measured in gsm, or grams per square metre.

Contacts

Alan Dye Associates
+44 (0)961 303 579

Area
+44 (0)171 354 0609

Artomatic
+44 (0)181 896 6666

Atelier Works
+44 (0)171 284 2215

The Attik
+44 (0)181 749 8090

Azone & Associates
+81 3 5411 0336

Bell
+44 (0)171 740 1414

Billy Mawhinney
+44 (0)171 240 4111

Birgit Eggers
+31 20 420 6198

Blast
+44 (0)171 242 9565

Carnegie Orr
+44 (0)171 610 6140

Conran Design Group
+44 (0)171 566 4566

Factor Design
+49 40 432 5710

The Foundry
+44 (0)171 734 6925

Frost Design
+44 (0)171 490 7994

Funny Garbage
+1 212 343 2534

Glazer Design
+44 (0)171 221 2595

Graphic Metal Company
+44 (0)1932 254 6699

HDR Design
+44 (0)1732 875 200

HGV
+44 (0)171 278 4449

Interbrand Newell & Sorrell
+44 (0)171 722 1113

Intro
+44 (0)171 637 1231

io360
+1 212 604 0543

Jaques Russell
+44 (0)171 437 4495

johnson banks
+44 (0)171 351 7734

Lippa Pearce
+44 (0)181 744 2100

Martin Perrin
+1 212 941 0700

MetaDesign
+44 (0)171 520 1000

Odermatt & Tissi
+41 1 211 9477

The Partners
+44 (0)171 608 0051

Pentagram
+44 (0)171 229 3477

Pyott Design
+44 (0)1883 627 627

Roundel Design
+44 (0)171 221 1951

Sagmeister Inc.
+1 212 647 1789

Sayles Design
+1 515 243 2922

Segura Inc.
+1 773 862 5667

Struktur Design
+44 (0)171 833 5626

Studio Myerscough
+44 (0)171 814 9125

Thomas Manss & Company
+44 (0)171 722 3186

The Typography Workshop
+44 (0)171 490 4386

Viva Dolan
+1 416 923 6355

Werner Design Works
+1 612 338 2550

Wild & Frey
+41 1 280 0898

Reading list
For a field of graphic design
practice that many designers
overlook in favour of the more
glamourous areas of poster design,
magazine and Web site design, it
is interesting to note that many of
the most influential designers and
design critics of the last century
have thought and written on the
subject. Below is a list of texts,
some of which are now out of
print, dealing with stationery
design and related subjects.

'Letters from the Avant Garde'
    Ellen Lupton and
    Elaine Lustig Cohen
    Princeton Architectural Press,
    1996

'Design Coordination and
Corporate Image'
    FHK Henrion and Alan Parkin,
    Reinhold Publishing Corp,
    New York, 1967

'The Graphic Designer and His
Design Problems'
    Josef Müller-Brockmann
    Hastings House, New York
    1971

'A History of Visual
Communication'
    Josef Müller-Brockmann,
    Hastings House, New York,
    1983

'The New Typography'
    Jan Tschichold, translated by
    Ruari McLean with an
    introduction by Robin Kinross,
    University of California Press,
    1995

'Design in Business Printing'
    Herbert Spencer,
    Thames & Hudson, 1952

'The Letterhead: History and
Progress'
    Ernst Lehner,
    Museum Books, New York,
    1955

'Paperwork'
    Nancy Williams,
    Phaidon Press, 1993

'Corporate Identity'
    Wally Olins,
    Thames & Hudson, 1995

Acknowledgements
An initial thank you to all of the
designers who submitted work for
inclusion in this book.

Thanks and IOUs also go to those
who helped with hints, tips and
patient advice, and those I just
bothered when they probably had
better things to do. In no particular
order: Teal Triggs, Emily Dowlen,
Robin Kinross, Patrick Baglee,
Ellen Lupton, Ruari McLean,
Nigel Roche, Dr Sue Walker,
and Angie Patchell at RotoVision,
who trusted us when we said it
would be finished soon.

In the course of research I also
visited a few institutions whose
ability to provide resources for
independent study is constantly
put under threat by the barbarians
at the gate: thanks to St Bride
Printing Library, the British Library
and the V&A's National Art Library.

Thanks also to Elaine Lustig-
Cohen, for permission to
reproduce letterheads from her
own collection, without which
kind gesture I might have been
reduced to drawing them by hand.

On that note, a big thanks also to
Xavier Young for fine photography
throughout the book.

A final, and particular thank you
goes to Roger Fawcett-Tang and
Ben Tappenden at Struktur Design,
who not only did an excellent
job with the design of the book,
but also suggested areas for
consideration.

Chris Foges